MANAGEMENT MATURITY

Prerequisite to Total Quality

A. Keith Barnes

UNIVERSITY
PRESS OF
AMERICA

Lanham • New York • London

Copyright © 1994 by
University Press of America®, Inc.
4720 Boston Way
Lanham, Maryland 20706

3 Henrietta Street
London WC2E 8LU England

Library of Congress Cataloging-in-Publication Data

Barnes, A. Keith.
Management maturity : prerequisite to total quality /
A. Keith Barnes.
p.   cm.
Includes bibliographical references and index.
1. Management.   2. Personnel management.   I. Title.
HD31.B36834   1994   658—dc20   94–22125 CIP

ISBN 0–8191–9645–2 (cloth : alk. paper)
ISBN 0–8191–9646–0 (pbk. : alk. paper)

Acknowledgements

In a normal lifetime, if we are very fortunate, we are influenced significantly by a few special people in our progress, our maturation. I know that any personal growth I have experienced has come in large measure from the influence of a great many people: students, teachers, siblings, parents and children, friends and colleagues. But I must acknowledge, particularly, my older brother John, my first real mentor; and my wonderful wife Judy - my raison d'etre and my endless source of inspiration.

There's a little of all of these people in whatever I have become, but this book is dedicated to the memory of my greatest mentor, Jack Cole. He is the one person from whom I learned immeasurably and invaluably about business and work. And from Jack I also learned so very much about the more important things: about people and values, about philosophy and politics, about loyalty and commitment. Jack Cole had an ordinary life by most standards - but all who knew him well can verify that this was no ordinary man.

MANAGEMENT MATURITY:
Prerequisite to TQM

PREFACE

"Maturity" means different things to different people, and in differing contexts. For this book, however, there is a specific meaning. The fundamental idea of maturity as used here comes from a model of human behavior called the Transcendence Model, the authors/originators being Walt Boshear and Karl Albrecht. Their model depicts those who do mature transcending the "immature" states of Dependence and Independence to one of Enlightened Interdependence. The assumption is that simply aging, or the passage of time, is an insufficient determinant of maturity. That there is need for this form of transcendence so that acknowledgement of the extent and importance of interdependence can surface and mature interdependent behaviors will be manifest.

In all spheres of human activity there are very important ways in which this concept can be applied, in personal relationships, especially in marriage, in international relations, in family and community life, etc. But nowhere is it more important or does it have more applicability, than in organizational life and particularly for those in supervisory and managerial positions. The primary challenge for all such people is in building highly effective teams of "followers" who can not only function effectively as a member of the team, but who can also build bridges of cooperation with other units of the organization and with external constituents.

A recent book by Katzenbach and Smith, The Wisdom of Teams, points out the many advantages of this approach and is somewhat prescriptive about how to build effective teams, but in large organizations, and even in those of modest proportions, there are highly complex internal interfaces. These interfaces, and the associated behaviors of people working at or across them, present enough challenges for all managers - even those who are relatively mature. The natural difficulty in team building is exacerbated by individual and collective immaturity in the form of extreme dependency or independence of action and thought.

In a remarkable story of large scale progress, American business has recently found ways to build bridges of cooperation with their suppliers, their customers and even with their rivals. The global scene is one characterized by collaborative efforts of all kinds and the many varieties of "joint ventures" are becoming commonplace. It is ironic, though, that the wisdom of such interdependent activity across organizational boundary lines has not transferred to the challenges of improving the organization internally. Instead, within the organization, immaturity abounds and shows up, mostly, in the form of independent behaviors - even in people who are chronologically mature and who hold significant responsibility. We must find ways to build progress at the internal interfaces equivalent to that now being experienced between organizations.

This book attempts to address many of the underlying immaturities, in people at all levels in any organization. There are some especially egregious errors being made in the fundamental practice of management, and these are the focus of my prescriptions. There are some context-building components to the book, too, but these are offered for the purpose of helping readers realize two things about learning "how to manage." First, that academic theories and model building in university - level courses and books on management have considerable applicability. Second, that there are some serious problems - constraints - with academic theories and models, constraints which have prevented their being more useful. One of the objectives I seek in preparing this manuscript is to bridge the rather large gap which still exists between theory and the practice of management.

In making the case for maturity, as defined here, as a prerequisite for the successful application of TQM (or any other management methodology) I must also caution that there is an even more fundamental prerequisite: in any organizational setting we must find ways to rekindle the enthusiasm of workers on all levels. The good news on this one, however, is that many of the prescriptions for building enthusiasm and commitment are also directly usable in building maturity. In fact all of the prescriptions delivered here have the power, if collectively applied, to create a strong culture of commitment and, at the same time, establish vital foundations for building maturity. In turn, this fortified foundation is an essential platform for launching any organizational thrust, such as TQM. In essence, this is akin to the ideals of building a contender in football. The basics of blocking and tackling must be mastered before elaborate team tactics and subtleties can be developed and applied successfully.

It is my starting assumption that you can build maximal commitment, and then maturity in your organization, by applying the several edicts which are contained and explained in this manual. I know that if you consistently apply these "rules" to your own behaviors, and seek to develop similar responses in others, your organization will improve and your career progress will also be enhanced. Management is difficult work . . . but it can be made much less difficult in an environment characterized by maturity.

INTRODUCTION

This book is written with one central assumption about all managers, that each really serves in three major roles (and many minor roles, of course):

SUPERVISOR; PEER; SUBORDINATE.
(I find the first and last of these terms abhorrent!)

To be truly effective in any organization one must learn how to BE these three entirely different people, and the many sub-roles within each of them. At various times, the behaviors discussed in the book relate to one or more of the three key roles, and, especially, to the implicit inter-dependencies. It is most important that you correctly apply the concepts to each of your roles and that you develop a high level of consciousness of your interactive role behaviors. All of this is going to be dealt with on an entirely personal level, it is assumed that you will find a way to particularize all suggestions and discussion to your own life and setting.

Skeptics may wonder how a "universal" set of prescriptions or edicts can apply in the many and varied settings of organizational life... and there certainly are huge differences between (say) the engineering department of a large aerospace defense contractor and the buying department of a retail enterprise...or....? All I can tell you is that the behavioral principles certainly do not change and that it is up to YOU to make the interpretation for your own setting. I will try, in the text, to identify critical externalities which play significant part in influencing behaviors and will also attempt to deal with the various "political" realities.

In all sections of the book there is explicit and implicit connection to the concept of MATURITY. Again, for purposes of this manual, maturity is a state (reached by some) in which there is constant acknowledgement of, and respect for, all inter-dependencies. Mature behaviors then are those which reflect this vigilance.

The General Structure of the Book

Each chapter or section will discuss practical do's and don'ts of management with implication from many different perspectives. Specific guidelines (and edicts) will be offered for dealing with the more important issues of management. In some of the chapters there will be sections each rather like an "aside" containing theoretical expansion or underpinning. In addition, near the end of the book (actually in Appendix A) you will find notes about some suggested readings apart from the selected references. In the Appendix B there is a case study presented to illustrate many of the principles and suggestions/edicts contained within the main body of text. It is a fictional story written specially for inclusion in this manual, but the behaviors exhibited in the story do happen in the "real world" and, in fact, most of the situations in the case are based on similar occurrences I have personally witnessed. There is an analysis of the case story to help readers come to understand potential outcomes of management immaturity; the analysis is supplemented by several prescriptions for prevention or alleviation of the dysfunctions evident in the case story.

There is a brief epilogue in which I try to make some final points about human resources and effective organization. I also add a few comments from other authors, to try to bolster these final claims.

TABLE OF CONTENTS

Chapters		Pages

Figure 1 The Maturation Model of Transcendence

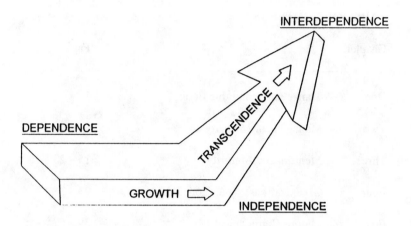

The Maturation Model, above, shows growth from the immature state of dependence through an intermediate and partly mature phase of independence, then transcendence to the fully mature state of interdependence. This model is adapted from two prior sources: "The Transcendence Theory" in The 1972 Annual Handbook for Group Facilitators by J. W. Pfeiffer & J. E. Jones (Eds.). Copyright @ 1972 by Pfeiffer & Company, San Diego, CA.: and Understanding People: Models and Concepts, by Walt Boshear and Carl Albrecht (1977), University Associates, Publisher, copyright @ by Cygni, Inc., Rancho Santa Fe, CA.

CHAPTER 1

Management and this Book

There are so many books on the market which attempt to provide "how-to" help for managers, and many of them are of some real value. . . then why another?

Many books on management seem to be withdrawn from where the action of management is, on a really personal level. Instead, they tend to be "macro-focused" on the organization as an abstraction. Or else they focus on the actions, decisions and roles of only the top two or three executives and "the big picture." The One Minute Manager was an exception, but one that was based on too narrow (though entirely valid) a construct. I will attempt to justify my opinion on this by delivering a larger operating framework in the pages of this manual; though one I admit also has its own limitations.

One of the most compelling of publications of the type which addressed the "big picture," Peters & Waterman's In Search Of Excellence, had so much of value to offer a practicing high-level manager, yet somehow missed many of the specific day to day personal do's and don'ts of effective management. The truth is that only a very small number of managers are really in genuine "strategic" positions. I acknowledge that all management should be strategic or have strategic implications, but for the vast majority of managers what is needed is not so much a treatise on how organizations are, or become, effective but more urgent, more specific and certainly more "personal" suggestions. Suggestions which actually show how to conduct oneself in those everyday challenges that all managers must face, ones which can help in the all-important effort to build highly committed and fully inter-dependent teams. An organization (or a football team) becomes effective when the majority of people involved are highly committed most of the time, and all are pulling together. Yes, strategic choices can be critical; but good strategic choices are necessary, though not sufficient. Some of the additional factors are dealt with here.

I must acknowledge the existence of many "complete" treatments of the subject of Management, the textual and teaching support materials used in colleges and universities everywhere. In the last three decades a great deal has been learned through research and experience about the highly complex nature of organizational leadership and decision making. Almost one in four of today's American college graduates major in business or a closely related discipline. Virtually all of these students will have worked with textual materials (and so, also, will a significant number of other people) which comprehensively present a full range of theoretical information ABOUT management. I tell my students that in college courses we learn ABOUT management, NOT HOW TO MANAGE. There is a huge difference, though there is an obvious connection, and this book attempts to make that nexus. My rationale for this book lies partly in the fact that formal (classroom based) education in management is substantially removed from the every day activities and interactions of practicing managers. But, at the same time, I feel that there are some theoretical materials which can be used to add meaning and understanding to some very real and directly usable guidelines. In this book, the theory and the practical are combined, with emphasis on a theoretical collective called MATURITY (please see the front materials).

Regrettable also, is that Schools of Business in America tend to place so much emphasis on what I call "The Rational Model" (TRM), though there are some powerful reasons for this emphasis. The most important reason is that many of the subjects which address organizational attempts to improve are quantifiable, with specific facts that are objectified, codified and institutionalized. In other words they are more or less rational. But as Nobel Laureate Herb Simon observed, there are limits (boundaries) to the rational process of decision making. While it is true that a smart manager does not make an important decision without first identifying the problem, considering and weighing alternatives according to some meaningful criteria, then making THE CHOICE (the TRM), there are so many occasions when such a process, in it's totality, is not only invalid but can be counterproductive.

Organizations are complex collections of people, improperly (I feel) defined as "working toward common goals." It is my contention that commonality of purpose is, or can become, an <u>outcome</u> of good management NOT a guiding light for it. Interdependence and mutual commitment, exhibited in effective organizations, comes about as a result of strong cultural "glue" which emanates from all employees and their actions (or at least from major constituencies of such) when there is a climate which fosters commitment. As a manager, on any level, one can influence the gradual emergence of such a culture, or one can be a negative or neutral figure, it is literally a choice individuals can make.

Even the very successful <u>In Search of Excellence</u> received much criticism, one of the most damning being its lack of valid academic research as basis for its proclamations; or, more properly, flimsy connections made between the underlying theory and its application. There is a huge volume of research, and of course experience, which CAN be brought to bear on prescriptions for effective management. One of the not-so-humble objectives of this book is exactly that, to provide some specific guidelines for management maturity to dominate in situations faced by managers; and to do so based on the delicate combination of theory and practice. I make the attempt to "make sense" of managers' work, and to identify specific ways of thinking and acting that can make an individual a better manager and the organization more effective. I specifically aim at reduction in levels of frustration that come with uncertainty and with immature managerial behaviors. NOT, I hastily add, to do so in the pretense or ignorance that the few suggestions made here will cover all situations. It is my contention however that there are a few nearly universal rules which can make <u>more likely</u> the positive outcomes which will make you successful in your own career. Perhaps more importantly, embracing these rules and applying them consistently, will develop in you, and in those around you, a <u>culture</u> of commitment and maturity which will foster the development of its own rules for sustenance of that culture and, thus, will help your organization become a better place for all employees under your influence. Such a place is also an ideal platform from which to launch TQM or any other fine-tuning you may decide to adopt.

Workers are collections of complex beings with enormously interactive, yet relatively predictable, needs and wants; their satisfaction level, their creativity, their enthusiastic involvement in decisions and enactment processes are so much more important than making THE RIGHT decision. I argue that a relatively "poor" decision with heavy commitment from the team of workers who have to make it work is much more important than having a perfectly well thought out decision that can be considered fully rational. Actually, it has been my experience that there is seldom need to "go" with a poor decision, but I choose this exaggeration only to make the point. Perhaps more significantly, the quality of any decision is in its outcomes anyway, so finding a way to achieve something desirable is not simply contained within the decision itself.... rather the entire process is the key.

Another of the weaknesses of TRM is that it tends to inculcate a belief that to every problem there is A solution. A more likely "truth" is that there can be many workable solutions, any one of which will produce very desirable results, or progress, AND, more importantly, if there can be a sense of participation and enthusiastic involvement by a large contingent of leader/followers not only will THAT decision turn out to be productive, but the environment engendered will foster the continued flow of ever better ideas and processes.

In the following chapters and pages of this book I attempt to show how, in ways applicable to virtually all situations, to build enthusiastic support among subordinates and fellow workers, though this is certainly a terrible oversimplification. One cannot apply them, in "One Minute" - but   nevertheless the concepts are relatively straight forward. I rely very heavily upon my personal experiences (read "mistakes") as a manager, and, because I know that ever increasing numbers of managers have been exposed to a growing body of management theory, I show, in some instances and especially in building understanding of the foundational concept (MATURITY) in the early chapters, how the concepts relate to research and literature of the field. Actually, of several fields, for management is a truly eclectic practice. It is through the use of some of the products of my learned academic colleagues that I attempt to legitimize the bases for my recommendations. The "new" approach here is simply a reversal of the more customary or textbook approaches. It is relatively easy to find texts and readers which take theoretical propositions and try to PUSH them into pedagogical fit with management practices. Here I use the opposite, less often tried approach: I deal with a variety of management roles and PULL appropriate theoretical or other literary materials into the scenario, for enlightenment and extension. In this way, I hope to achieve two things most important in learning: first, legitimization of the managerial experience not founded in theory, and second, building upon the strengths of each reader's own managerial experience and identity, by explaining such in theoretical terms.

I make no claim that all who read this book will become successes in the organizational world. Nor do I claim that (in fact I insist on emphasizing this shortcoming) this treatise is comprehensive. I do claim, however, that the principles and practices recommended are sound in theory and practice, and if they are carefully applied IN TOTAL then the results will be most satisfactory, and satisfying over the long haul. Most importantly, a solid basis for your continued maturation can be built, along with a base for the application of more complex organizational prescriptions.

This last point, which implies long term commitment, consistency and a great deal of patience, may well be the main Achilles heel of this approach to management. Ours is an impatient world, our systems of management and control tend to be inflexible, bureaucratic and, more importantly, force an unwillingness to wait for results before declaring a decision to be inappropriate. In fact one's very survival in a responsible position may well depend upon instant or early performance to standards and goals that can actually fly in the face of some of the concepts of the approach to management espoused here. But I'm an optimist, in spite of TRM and the competitive threats which all organizations must survive, I see a very slow evolution toward more values oriented management. I see the influence of Japanese management and similar admitted fads beginning to make themselves manifest. For the life of me I cannot fully understand what took us so long. . . the principles have been taught by American academics, in very academic ways, for nearly half a century. Never mind, though; if our organizations are even partly ready to admit to the need for human and mature approaches to management, there is hope. We will find, if we are to be maximally competitive on an international basis once again, that it will not be our technologies that propel us, nor our ability to apply the many aspects of TRM, but our ability to rekindle the enthusiasm and creativity of large numbers of our work force. Technological advances will follow such organizational improvement. Our human resources can and will find ways to deliver products and services at levels of quality and cost effectiveness if reward structures and environments of work are appropriate.

It may be entirely rewarding for a Toyota employee, in Japan, to begin his day (yes, Japan is still largely a male dominant society) singing the company song, and not so appropriate for his American counterpart, but for every individual and for every organizational culture there is a key. As a manager it may not be your responsibility to (using a phrase from the 60's) get inside the head of your employees, but it is your responsibility to find ways that the majority of your employees can become committed and enthusiastic, especially if such attitudes can propel the organization toward excellence and effectiveness as I believe they can.

Incidentally, before moving on I must attempt to "place" the concept of MANAGEMENT MATURITY in respect to other approaches and guidelines for business success. Readers in business, particularly, are likely to have been made aware of the many "trendy" business issues of recent years, including Total Quality Management (TQM). Despite arguments to the contrary TQM is little different, in my opinion, from Zero-Defects and many other fads of the last several decades. It (TQM) does, however, have a very broad base - goes way beyond just product quality - so it deserves a close look. But my approach to Maturity is a meaningful way of building total quality into the human organization with resultant progression to non-human aspects being the ultimate outcome. I remain convinced that product and service quality are an outcome of management maturity, one involving values and human qualities which must precede all attempts to develop other strengths and values. Hence the second part of my title: Prerequisite to TQM.

In the next chapter I discuss a few basic assumptions and theories which underlie, or partly explain what I label "Management Maturity." Subsequent chapters attempt to extend those basics to a variety of real-world situations and management challenges.

CHAPTER 2

Management Maturity and You

WHY DO WORKERS DO WHAT THEY DO?

The heading for this section is an old question that has been answered in a variety of ways - all the way from "economic man" to "self-actualization." But your own story may not be entirely unique, so why not try to get at your own motives, using your own work experience.

What is it about your work and/or your work situation that "turns you on?" Why are you prepared to go to the office, or take work home with you, and work without extra compensation until late in the evening or perhaps on the week-end? If you have the insight to be able to answer these questions then I have another for you: What makes you so different? Now here comes the tough part: the truth is, barring some sort of low probability event that really does make you different biologically . . . YOU are not DIFFERENT! You do what you do because when you do these things you derive some sort of satisfaction. Well everyone else has the same potential inner responses and motivations. The problem is that workers who do less than you do, or who are more interested in things other than their work, have been trained that way. In other words, incentives of a complex sort have served to shape their behaviors over a long period of time. Retraining of any behavior, yes including attitudes, for the majority of people, is not that far out of reach. While it may be dangerous to generalize about people, it can be useful. The good news about the application of this, and other theories useful in management, is that you do not have to be absolutely right all the time. Even in baseball a hitter who can safely hit one time out of three is extremely successful, most of those who hold their position on a big-league team are far less prolific than that!

Workers are incredibly forgiving. So long as you, or some things systemic in your organization, are not blocking their paths to reasonable levels of satisfaction (which result in frustration and turn-off) you do not have to be constantly reinforcing their appropriate behavior. A behavioral scientist would refer to this concept as inter-mittent reinforcement and it has been found that even in laboratory rats a "trained" pattern of behavior does not die out when reinforce-ment patterns are relatively sporadic or intermittent. So long as there are no unconscious (or unconsciously negative) reinforcers present then intermittent reinforcement is every bit as sustaining of a behavior as is continuous reinforcement. In simple terms this means that you can be really sloppy about recognizing performance some of the time so long as you are not perceived to be punishing the appropriate behavior or reinforcing (encouraging) inappropriate behaviors.

Incidentally, I have a somewhat unusual view of what is often referred to as a "human relations" approach to management. It is true that many people find satisfactions in a friendly environment in which appreciation is shown for accomplishments, good attitude, etc. Fred Hertzberg referred to these, among many others, as workplace hy-gienes. He asserted that such are important but not sufficient to "motivate" workers. Instead, people become energized by such things as challenge, growth, opportunity and their own sense of accom-plishment. Good human relations under these assumptions are posi-tive conditions, but ask yourself this question: Would you rather work in an environment in which management is pleasant, apprecia-tive, and respectful of your human dignity, or where such factors are not in evidence, but you feel constantly stimulated by new challenges, each building on the prior, and where you feel that you are trusted to create new approaches and even make mistakes? The truth is - I have asked hundreds of people this question - that mature people prefer the latter...to be challenged in ways which match their ability and readi-ness. Your job as a manager is to help people mature to the point where this is the preference for most of the workers and for most that the level of challenge is rising. There is absolutely no reason to abandon a "human relations" environment in the process, by the way. These are not mutually exclusive desirables, thus if you apply both you get the benefits which come from each.

Work itself, under ideal circumstances, can be wildly exciting! Think back to something you did, on your own, or with others, that you found totally absorbing or interesting. Can you think of something? Can you describe what it was that MADE it so exciting? Can you find ways to make everyone under your influence more excited about what they do?

The sad fact is that much work is not inherently stimulating and does not particularly challenge the worker. In addition, the surrounding environmental conditions (including you, boss) present few reinforcements for the behaviors that you have personally made your habit and would want to see in your employees. Or worse, there are direct forms of frustration in the systems and the behaviors of superiors and co-workers. Incidentally, on the subject of commitment, if your OWN behaviors do not reflect high levels of commitment and enthusiasm then all bets are off. Take this book back to where you obtained it immediately and demand your money back! We may be able to tune-up your maturity, thus improving your ability to lead, but not if you lack the necessary commitment yourself.

Please note that throughout this book, or at least in Chapters Two though Nine, I will be delivering edicts which punctuate my suggestions. It is time for the first of these edicts:

EDICT No. 1:   IT IS NOT YOUR JOB TO TELL OTHERS
                 WHAT TO DO; OR HOW TO DO IT!

There are so many practicing managers who seem to have a false assumption about this. I have known several who literally spell words for their secretaries, or tell them how to address the letter and structure it, or have other similar tendencies. OK, so you are not one such. . . but, chances are that you do the equivalent, with other people, without realizing it, and you do it often.

Oh, as I said earlier, employees are very forgiving, and will tolerate an awful lot of your errors as a manager, and in fact, our culture has produced a grudging acceptance of this definition of a boss (one who tells us what to do and how to do it). Well, if it is not your job to tell workers what to do and how to do it, what is your job?

The answer is complex, and can only be revealed in the total treatment attempted throughout this book, but let me make a partial start by saying (deliberately oversimplifying, at this stage) that it is primarily your job to build a team of people who, themselves, most of the time, correctly identify what to do and how to do it, and get it done efficiently. Incidentally, efficiency should never be a primary objective, instead, a preferred primary objective is effectiveness, though I believe we should not abandon the notion of efficiency, only relegate it to a desirable outcome of effective operations. More on this topic later.

Before going further, we need to go a bit beyond the basics into a concept that I refer to as the MATCH-UP; and this is a good place for the next edict. . .

EDICT No. 2:   IT IS YOUR JOB TO CREATE WORK-RELATED MATCH-UPS.

Let's use the analogy of a child, say eight or ten years old, and create a scenario: the parent of the child allows him, sitting in Dad's, lap to "drive" the family car on a public road. Some would argue that this is a relatively harmless way to get the child to realize the excitement and responsibility of driving, or to get "closer" to the parent. I contend that it is a wild mismatch between maturity and responsibility. Most of us would not indulge a small child in this way. Some might refrain because it is against the law, or because there is personal risk. The best reason for not doing this, however, is that the child develops a false sense of whom and what he is and his role. Precocious behavior is not a pretty sight! Neither is discouragement and withdrawal, even if disguised, as they so often are. The child who is not permitted some slight experiments relatively close to matching, but beyond his/her maturity, is going to be discouraged and underdeveloped if this is the dominant control model by the parents. Am I implying that parenting is a form of management? You bet I am! There are important distinctions to be made, but many similarities. One of the major distinctions is that workers are legally "mature" before they come under your influence. They are also responsible, not just for their own well-being, but also for their own continuing growth and maturation. Your role then, is to provide the kind of appropriate challenges and opportunities which will stretch them and kindle their enthusiasm for what they do and how they do it. Why not just give them an assignment which will help you meet your goals? Because that will merely ensure (for most workers) a low level of commitment and a serious missed opportunity for the whole organization.

THEORY BASE (Reader: Skip these parts if you wish)

I hope that you can get used to these injections and that you will not see them as intrusions? My purpose after discussing a particular topic will be to generalize and discuss the theory and/or research that is behind the topic. If you wish, you may skip these sections and simply concentrate on the prescriptive portions, but I believe that an understanding of the theory will help you to apply the concepts in a variety of situations. It will also be useful in teaching others, a most important part of the managerial responsibility. For those who believe that this is inconsistent with edict No. 1, I'll explain: for me, teaching is not telling! Instead, teaching is providing an environment, stimuli, and reinforcement for the learning process to blossom.

In the foregoing section there was reference to a number of concepts that need explanation and expansion. Essentially we are dealing with the behavioral concept of MOTIVATION, to which there are several sub-topics.

The motivation to work, according to many theorists, is as basic to the human as is the motivation to eat and sleep. It is seen as a complex need and it is useful to examine it in light of an hierarchy of complex human needs, as proposed by Abraham Maslow. There are, according to Maslow, many different kinds of human needs and they tend to drive behavior in attempts to satisfy the need in question. Essentially a satisfied need no longer has the same capacity to direct behavior as one that is not satisfied (when we are not hungry we will not behave in ways that relate to hunger, for example). The Maslow hierarchy of needs includes five levels, each successively more complex than the one preceding it and these needs (types) are:

Lowest Level
> Basic, or Physiological Needs. Including the need for food, air, water, sleep, physiological warmth (and maybe sex, too, but this is controversial; some arguing that sex is a social need - see below).

Second Level
> Safety needs. Including shelter, and the avoidance of physiological discomfort or threat.

Third Level
> Social needs. Including touch, interaction and belonging or acceptance.

Fourth Level
> Ego needs. Including recognition, achievement, and success.

Fifth Level
> Self Actualization. Including growth, stimulation, challenge and fulfillment.

The important point of the Maslow need hierarchy is that only the unsatisfied needs serve to drive current behavior AND that the lowest level of unsatisfied need is predominant in behavior. One can readily see that if you are hungry (thirsty, or cold, or . . .?) there is little point someone trying to entice you to do something for which the reward is recognition, for example. After your more basic need is satisfied, however, then just maybe . . . Also, remember that, like hunger, any need that is satisfied is only satisfied for the duration, it will recur.

A fly in the ointment of this and all motivation theories is that satisfied people are evidently not motivated, at least not maximally! In other words, if we have an objective of creating opportunities for workers to achieve satisfaction, they will be relatively lethargic if we are successful. In fact, the many attempts to test the notion that job satisfaction leads to high productivity, have failed to show such a connection, or can at least be challenged for one reason or another. As a matter of fact, the cause-effect relationship is never proven and the reverse dependency IS sometimes shown: <u>that feelings of productivity lead workers to feelings of satisfaction with their job!</u> Many management theorists, for these reasons, advocate creating an environment in which people feel successful, most of the time. I agree with this objective and believe the approaches described in this book will produce such results. The problem with "satisfaction" is that it has many hard to define aspects. Certainly as used in laboratory research (a recently well-fed rat is described as being satisfied), there is not much we can do with the construct, directly.

The human animal is very complex, and can undoubtedly find, or invent, complex chains of satisfactions, but one useful way to think of individuals, in connection with the Maslow hierarchy of needs, is in terms of MATURITY. This, too, is a difficult concept, but imagine workers who are "operative" at the lowest levels of the hierarchy, needing from their work those things which protect them and provide for their (non-private) needs and wants at a very fundamental level. Such people can be thought of as immature, though they may be of any chronological age. For those who are operative at higher levels, the basics are no longer satisfactory and they need to receive "rewards" that are more complex, and in this sense, they are more mature.

I will come back to this concept many times in future sections because it is rather important and has to do with dealing with people "where they are," or the MATCH-UP requirement that I mentioned earlier. It is one thing to have a basic understanding of this concept, and quite another to learn how to recognize signs of "maturity." In later sections of this book we will examine some specific ways of identifying signs of maturity and of helping people to progress to ever more mature levels.

There are many other theories of motivation, but this particular one, Maslow's, and a couple of others, are intrinsic theories because they are based on the premise that we humans have inner directions for our behavior, inner needs which we constantly seek to satisfy. It is critical to note that these theories do not suggest that external factors, even rewards, are motivating. Instead the motivations themselves are internal. This has important implications for managers because implicit is the limitation that external factors (and people) cannot motivate, merely encourage or discourage certain behaviors!

I illustrate the importance of this last point (in my classes) by setting up a classical conditioning experiment with a hungry rat in a

(Skinner) box. We are attempting to "shape" certain simple behaviors by rewarding the rat, with food pellets, when behaviors approximate (initially) the desired behavior. I ask the students what motivates the rat to do the behavior and invariably the instinctive reply is: "the food pellet." Absolutely the wrong answer! The rat is motivated by its own need (hunger) for food! Try training a recently well-fed rat and you find the evidence for this claim. It must be acknowledged that hunger, unlike some more complex (higher-order) needs, has a relatively narrow range of options for satisfaction; and that the rat is a relatively simple organism, but you get the point.

You may well have heard of people who are referred to as "great motivators," however proponents of intrinsic theories would point out that the behavior is inner directed and that only the rewards come from outside. This means that the so-called motivator has simply been associated with the desired rewards and has found a way to provide valued rewards systems on a consistent basis. I would suggest to you that a good manager must find a way to do precisely these things AND to deal with people WHERE THEY ARE! That is managers must find reinforcement approaches, for appropriate behaviors, that satisfy the operant needs of the employees, as individuals. It is pretty obvious that an employee with the lowest levels of need unsatisfied is not going to respond well to a rewards system that addresses self actualization needs. By contrast a worker who has been living well for some time (has basic, or first-level needs largely filled) who has a full social life and is well adjusted and has a basically unselfish attitude CANNOT be rewarded by anything other than that which addresses self-actualization needs.

The result of appropriate work place match-ups of the sort prescribed in the foregoing is high levels of commitment and a readiness for maturity. The result of mismatches, that is too little or too much challenge, is frustration. We must acknowledge that human behavior is complex, particularly in a work setting, and the identification of operant needs and suitable reward mechanisms are very difficult. In later chapters we will attempt some illumination on this important and foundational concept, in our pursuit of the keys to mature and effective leadership and management.

The next chapter is devoted to the theory and practical values of Mentoring, a special responsibility for all mature managers.

CHAPTER 3

Mentors and Maturity

One of the most beneficial relationships we can experience, especially for our professional development, is that involving a mentor. As a matter of fact I am so narrow minded on this one that I believe that no-one can become a truly effective manager without having had at least one, and probably several, relationship with a true mentor.

A mentor does much more than just teach, though that too may be involved, and even the dictionary definition hardly does the concept justice: "A wise and trusted counselor." The truth is that wisdom is a relative thing, and to a fool most others have wisdom, though the fool may not know it! At each stage of one's personal development we need opportunity to reflect on our own philosophy and mission... we even need some source of inspiration from which we develop a concept of mission. If we grow and our mentors do not grow beyond our own new level then the future benefits from that same mentor must decline. In my own life I can think of no less than five mentors who have been of enormous impact upon my personal and professional development, one of whom I single out in opening pages of this book. Let us see if we cannot penetrate the real significance of the mentor relationship in terms that relate to what has been presented so far.

Your mentors must generally have conformed to some or all of the following specific behaviors and influences. First, they must have MADE YOU FEEL WORTHWHILE. It is highly probable that you have learned a great deal from a large number of people in your life, yet many of them could not be regarded as mentors. It is also true that any real relationship with others involves development of mutual "worthwhile" feelings. This is the case with friendship and certainly with a good marriage. However, true mentors (and indeed some individuals in other relationships) take their own rewards at very high levels of abstraction, and in many cases are altruists (hence the dictionary definition "trusted") and receive great satisfaction from giving. In such giving, without conditions, just as in any true love relationship, the recipient feels most significant. If you yourself are under operant motivation levels that demand your own giving, instead of receiving, then you are ready to be an advanced mentor yourself. And, of course, one can be mentor in one relationship and at one level, yet a protege in another. In the workplace, the feelings of being worthwhile can certainly extend beyond your professional worth, and often do, but the work-related worthwhile awareness must be present.

Your mentors must have made you INCREASINGLY AWARE OF YOUR OWN STRENGTHS. There are a great many ways we can learn of our own strengths. If we are tested in a certain way, and we overcome, undoubtedly we learn that we can accomplish whatever was involved in that challenge. Regrettably we rarely come to understand ourselves the way others do, and a mentor who has insight and cares about us will help us get in touch with what we can accomplish. The human animal is so complex, however, and simply knowing what we can accomplish doesn't, on its own, stimulate the accomplishment. This is where the external influencers play a role. The significance of the increasing aspect of this is most critical; strengths change as we grow, they are not of a static nature or importance. Some strengths dissolve and are replaced, others continue to develop and expand. Your mentor is the catalyst for the understanding of this change.

Your Mentors will have FOUND WAYS FOR YOU TO STRETCH. When we are small children learning some of the very simple survival type skills such as how to feed ourselves and how to speak, we have tremendously powerful motivations. If we are hungry, or thirsty, we stretch our communicative skills constantly until we learn how to ask for help in obtaining food and drink. Our parents, along with our own (inner directed) needs provide opportunity and instruments for stretching our ability. If we examine the typical learning curve for growth in just one area, language ability, we find extremely fast growth from age two, approximately (when our neurological maturation first permits such development), to about the age of ten or twelve. By then we will typically have learned as much as half our lifetime vocabulary, unless we later learn a new language. By age twenty-five, our rate of new language skills will have slowed almost to a standstill, though none of us will master our native language. The main reason for the slowing growth rate is that once we can "get by" we no longer feel the need to stretch that ability so powerfully. When we do make concerted efforts to grow in some specific way there is usually someone (or perhaps some situation) which pressures us to stretch. This is indicative of some peculiarly human trait which need not be discussed here except to say that a mentor just has that insight and the ability to go beyond helping us recognize our strengths and finds a way to stretch us just beyond our present capacity. In his(her) influence, the continued growth, and the excitement from such, remains an aggressive stimulus.

Your mentor NEVER LET YOU DOWN. Of course human frailties are real and plentiful and anytime we place someone on a pedestal there is always the danger that they could fall from grace in some way because of a human weakness. Real mentors somehow remain above reproach in a sordid world. Some say that our world is deteriorating but I'm not really convinced that our world is any more sordid than it ever has been, and feel quite certain that the majority of people are honest and live decent lives. Certainly those who can be defined this way are the population from which mentors must come and then, since their own motives are unselfish, they will be less likely to indulge in behaviors which could cause you disappointment. If you have mentors in your past, and if you still remember their contributions to your lifetime development in positive ways, it is no doubt because they did nothing (or little) to diminish your respect for them.

In spite of the importance of this one, I must add a caveat. As we mature, we become more circumspect about human frailty. A small child who discovers a failing in a parent is likely to be very upset by the realization. By contrast, an adult is much more likely to accept the same failing. So it is with our mentors of our adulthood. In addition, as we ourselves mature, we are much more likely to accept the reality that our mentors do not provide for us all the positive influences we need in any event. In other words we accept that none of us is "complete," and this helps us come to understand our own frailty. If, as they say, "life begins at forty," it is because, at about that age, if ever, we finally come to accept our own human limitations and those of others. It does not mean that we stop caring about continued growth, however! Your mentors WERE AVAILABLE TO YOU BUT NEVER SOLVED YOUR PROBLEMS FOR YOU. There is a great tendency among many of us to see a cry for help as a request for someone else to do our problem-solving for us. Parents tend to make this mistake with small children and, all too often, with large children too. Politicians also base much of their thinking on this same assumption, with constituents, resulting in ever growing and ever more paternalistic central governments. This tendency in government may well produce a response in the population for greater dependence, less maturity. Managers also make this same mistake, but your genuine mentor, instead, permitted you the luxury and freedom to make mistakes all of your own, always under a watchful but never paternal eye, and surprise, surprise, you made fewer mistakes as time went by.

In summary, then, you get better, more complete under the influence of a real mentor. Not because he/she did anything to you or for you, but because YOU . . . .

a) Felt worthwhile;

b) Knew your strengths and felt the growth;

c) Felt the exhilaration that comes with challenge;

d) Knew that human existence embraces an ethical value system;

e) Knew that help and encouragement was available, always.

Right now, why don't you write down on a sheet of paper the name(s) of your mentors. Next to each name write an acknowledgement about each of the above listed mentoring factors and then identify at least one particular example for each of the characteristics that you can recall, these will serve to verify that this was a true mentor relationship.

Next, whether or not your mentor is still alive, write a letter to him or her, a very brief letter expressing your feelings and gratitude for your development as a human, and for their significance in that growth. If the mentor in question is alive, mail the letter! If not, keep the letter handy for future (often) reference.

This last suggestion is not my attempt to be pious but is based on an understanding that you must take overt steps in cementing your own feelings of what benefits came to you in a mentor relationship. For you to become a really good manager you must elevate your relationships to ensure that you are a mentor to your own people.

Next, dig deep into your recent memory of behaviors with other people in the work setting. Identify the specific behaviors of yourself and others. Write down in brief the genuine mentoring activities observed in others and those committed by you. Also, identify all the recent missed opportunities for appropriate mentoring behaviors. Try to identify what prevented the appropriate behavior on your part. You may want to refer back to these missed opportunities when you come to Chapters eight and nine.

THEORY BASE

At the turn of this century, a century or more after the industrial revolution got rolling, there had been very little thought given to management, as a concept. The truth is that until advanced forms of mechanization and large complex organizations emerged, there really was no such thing as a separate management class, and really no such thing as a middle-class either. It had become apparent, however, that bringing large numbers of workers together did create a whole new category of supervisory problems unlike anything in prior human experience. It is evident that many in the upper classes certainly had little concern for employees, and there had been little need for a special class of workers (managers) taking on responsibility for large numbers of others. The military has always been a special exception, itself an example of two classes to this day (enlisted and commissioned).

With the work of an industrial engineer, Frederick Taylor, and a few others with similar convictions (labeled, later the Scientific Management movement) came the notion that a manager's responsibility was to define and monitor the work of non-managers. This ultimately led to such concepts as "time and motion study" and probably had a great deal to do with increased emphasis on labor unions.

Continued attempts to get more productivity from workers, to match that of the mechanized areas of production, led to all kinds of workplace studies. Scientific method, as applied to social/behavioral situations was also just blossoming and, under the supervision of Elton Mayo a group of researchers from Harvard College (Roethlisberger & Dickson, 1939) began a series of experiments at the Western Electric plant at Hawthorne, near Chicago. These studies, which took place in the 1920's were to become landmarks in what we now label "The Human Relation Movement," though I feel strongly that this is a misnomer, for reasons I discussed earlier. The researchers themselves never did really understand what it was that they discovered, though they spent many years trying to reach some supported conclusions... hence the publication date nearly a decade after the experiments were completed. The authors spent a great deal of time, as have countless academics since, trying to uncover the real meaning of the Hawthorne findings.

At Hawthorne, various groups of manual workers were carefully measured in their productivity as a function of many variables. Original areas of interest, such as plant lighting level, temperature, etc., were expanded to include a wide variety of "independent variables" including Supervisory Style. Because we now know that workers (or subjects in any experiment) who know they are being observed behave differently from "normal," all findings were suspect and confusing. By the way, we now label this the "Hawthorne Effect," a very serious challenge in all social research. One of the major confusions at Hawthorne came from a finding of increased productivity after light levels were reduced!

Recent interpretations of findings at Hawthorne most often stress the significance of group relatedness as a satisfier and motivator. There is not much doubt that group involvement is a fundamental need (a social need) for most people. A less often cited independent variable, and one I personally stress, is the need for feelings of social, or workplace significance.

There is not much doubt in my mind that workers such as those in the Hawthorne Experiments were made to feel rather significant, often for months at a time, as their particular unit was under surveillance by the research team and members of management. Remember, this was the late 1920's, present day working conditions and assumptions about rights, etc., are quite different; though underlying principles are the same.

Why do I include this account here, after discussing mentoring? Well, first of all, these particular research efforts, and the decades-long attempts to evaluate results, really underpin all modern management theory. They were really that significant. Additionally, my emphasis on worthwhile feelings are directly related to the first requirement for all mentor relationships*.

Before moving ahead, and while still discussing theory, I must now confuse the issue, slightly, by informing readers that there is yet another relevant, and most important, meaning for Maturity. Chris Argyris (Behavioral Scientist) devised a model of human maturity with seven dimensions. He concluded that we mature along seven independent dimensions, at different rates for each dimension, as we grow toward adulthood:

1) Passive behaviors become more active;

2) Dependence is replaced with independence;

3) A narrow range of behaviors becomes broad, complex;

4) Shallow interests deepen, or are replaced with deep ones;

5) Short time perspectives become longer;

6) Subordinacy changes and we feel equal or superior;

7) Self awareness and self control develop.

Argyris says that we progress on these seven dimensions, as we mature. The dimension I wish to stress here, though some of the others are also relevant, is that of dependence/independence. While it

---

* The history of mentoring is much older than the Hawthorne Studies, of course, going all the way back to Greek Mythology. Mentor was the trusted friend of Odysseus, whose son, Melachus, was "Mentored." Though there is much applied study of modern mentoring, little fundamental research on the subject exists.

is true that independence is one sure sign of maturation, I contend that we further transcend a state of independence, at least in some aspects of our behavior, to INTER-DEPENDENCE. Later, as we shall see, this leads us to Systems Theory, and other advanced topics, but for now, let me stress the importance of inter-dependence, especially for the acknowledgement of inter-dependence, for individuals in the workplace. The model (diagram) of Boshear and Albrecht, shown in the front materials, should be examined very carefully. Please note that this is not the only model which relates maturity to interdependence - there are many others I could have selected. The connection between these two concepts, however, is central to everything contained in these pages. As John Donne said, nearly four centuries ago, "No Man Is An Island entire unto himself. . ." He was so right, but especially is this so in the workplace, and especially in the complex organization. There are many ways that this reality impacts management thinking and decision-making, but for now, while working with the contents of this chapter, let us just acknowledge that the role of the mentor/manager is, in part, helping all employees mature in this sense. That is in moving beyond dependency, through stages of independent thought and action to a productive and cooperative state of inter-dependence and mutual beneficiation.

Before leaving the discussion of inter-dependence let me stress one caveat: Theorists developing this notion assert, and I tend to agree, that it is virtually impossible to go directly to mature (inter-dependent) states without first experiencing the less mature or more selfish state of independence. This being the case, mentors can play a most significant role in helping proteges through the intermediate stage. Many interpersonal conflicts in the workplace are caused, directly and indirectly, by the selfish acts of the chronically independent. In some situations it is easier to deal with the consequences of dependence than with the highly independent. Much more will be done with this concept in later chapters.

With these initial practical edicts and theoretical underpinnings now understood, we are ready to move forward into some topics related to your supervisory role and to that of peer. Chapter Four will attempt to acknowledge and describe the influences of a confusing array of organizational variables. Some of these variables you may not be in a position to control or change, but all of them tend to make the waters of management very murky indeed.

CHAPTER 4

Organizational Variables Affecting You and Your People

In the preceding chapters I have discussed some aspects of organizational behavior as though I believe that all individuals are more or less the same. I have stressed variance in <u>maturity</u>, with its different meanings, and leave out discussion of the many other variables and dimensions on the basis of which there is individual variance. I must now make it clear why I have taken this approach. It is simply that non-human factors in the organizational setting are, in many ways, very powerful, substantially unifying, and tend to have the effect of heavily tempering individual differences. The theoretical explanations for this are most closely related to group theory, which is introduced as part of this chapter and is also discussed further in Chapter 8. There are, I contend, some high probability assumptions about individuals in the work place which can provide a basis for good management decisions <u>most of the time</u>. As the rest of this book unfolds proper attention will be paid to ways in which, and circumstances under which, <u>circumstantial</u> differences force alternative approaches beyond my general edicts. The details of such circumstances and how to handle them are dealt with, especially, in Chapter Nine.

The problem of differences between organizational characteristics is of significance primarily in that you, as a manager, must come to terms with them as part of your decision process and in order to have even a chance of understanding individual behaviors. The reason for this is that the environment of the organization, and each sub-unit, provides much of the stimulus for behavior and also provides many frustrations which individuals experience. I will discuss some of the most significant organizational variables first,

24   *Organizational Variables*

then will deliver a small number of edicts which have nearly universal validity.

SIZE and STRUCTURE

Organizations vary in size and their structural form, of course. There is little doubt that the enormous differences of size (as measured by the number of people and the number of levels) are critical factors in determining a number of characteristics of organizational life and behavior. Confounding the issue is the fact that even among organizations of relatively equivalent size there are sub-variables which are also critical. The interactive effects between these factors and size produce a bewildering combination of possible organization types. To the degree that you can, from your level of engagement, you must come to terms with these characteristics so that you can predict certain happenings with some degree of reliability. Why? Because your followers need to feel the confidence that comes from such abilities AND you need to protect your people from the ravages of aberrant happenings, as much as possible.

I hope that this does not convey a paternalistic attitude; far from it. We must, as mature managers, encourage people on every level to face uncertainty and turbulence as part of their maturation. But the kind of "aberrant happenings" to which I refer are those which confuse, discourage and frustrate and therefore constrain individual growth/maturity. I will try to show some distinctions as we progress.

The sub-organizational variables of greatest significance are:

Degree of Centralization;

The Degree of Bureaucracy;

The Dominant Power Culture;

The Rate of Technological Change;

The Homogeneity of Product and Process;

The Nature of the Structural Inter-dependencies.

CENTRALIZATION

There are two different meanings to this concept, and both are important. First, an organization which is located all in one building, or in relatively close geographic locations, is one that can be called "Centralized." It usually means that lines of communication are short and sub-cultures relatively homogeneous. Be careful with this generalization, however, and see (especially) the sections on product homogeneity and structural interdependency, below.

It is time to take a brief side trip into theoretical understandings of "Culture." If we examine a dictionary definition of this term, we will find reference to behaviors which distinguish a group, such as: language, dress, comportment, religious practices, family practices, etc. The closedness of a culture, that is its tendency to remain separate from other cultures, is, in large measure dependent on two things: the strength of the overall commitment to a majority of the unique cultural characteristics; and the degree of perceived difference between the majority of characteristics and those of another culture with which contact is possible. In an organization setting, there are "cultural" differences between operating departments and divisions because each sub-unit has language, customs and perspectives which differ from those of other sub-units.

Just as in the social world, physical closeness alone is not sufficient to break down barriers when the sub-cultural differences are clearly in evidence and strongly adhered to. The Accounting Department, the Production Department and the Sales Department of a manufacturing firm (as examples) are destined to be in conflict by the nature of their different cultures. Exacerbating this fact is the likelihood that few people in any of these departments automatically feel strongly compelled to come to understand the nature of any other department's problems.

We refer to this as structurally based latent conflict. The degree to which conflict is actually manifest depends very much on several interactive factors:

a) The overall degree of success/failure in meeting objectives;

b) The perceived levels of interference by "other" departments in meeting sub-unit goals;

c) The scarcity of resources and the degree of competition for those resources;

d) The MATURITY (surprise, surprise!) of the leadership;

e) The maturity of others in all the various sub-units or departments in acknowledging interdependence.

Now, back to your role in dealing with the vagaries of these realities, let me deliver the next edict.

EDICT No. 3:   BE PREPARED TO CROSS THE CULTURAL BOUNDARIES IN A STATE OF OPENNESS . . .

and with a genuine interest in helping understand the "other" culture and their problems. This must be done when there are NO current manifest conflicts!

This is a rather lengthy edict but a most important one. Many (immature) managers, I find, are willing to contact the "others" to do one of several things:

a) Seek help in solving their own problems;

b) Attempt to convince the "others" of the critical nature of their own current dilemma;

c) To seek some support for a major change effort perceived by themselves to be in the vital interest of the firm.

This would be rather like Saddam Hussein visiting the Israeli Government to persuade them to provide funds to develop the Iraqi economy. No matter how critical the economic position of Iraq, or how Saddam might try to convince Israel that their cooperation would be in their own best interest, or that of the whole world, the effort is doomed to failure. Why? Because it is based on entirely the wrong assumptions for conflict resolution. Saddam can only make progress in relationships with Israel (or anyone with whom there is manifest or latent conflict) if he first shows a genuine desire in understanding Israel's problems and actually exhibits supportive behaviors in helping Israel solve them! Similarly, you must build your bridges with other organizational units all the time and not when you have a problem with which "they" can help you. How do you do this? Well, fortunately, organizations in which close proximity of all units is the reality (geographically centralized), there are some things going on which make it relatively easy for you. First of all, it is easier for you to be current on simple things like names and faces. But don't let this important work just happen. Go out of your way to acknowledge promotions and accomplishments outside your own department and to be generally interested and friendly. Get out of your office and meet that new whatever person, even if there is little chance of your needing help from that position, per se. It should by now be obvious why these "time wasters" are necessary. Incidentally, be absolutely certain that you do not, in fact, waste your (or the other person's) time in these visits, be brief, friendly and offer your help in their problems. MEAN IT!

Secondly, formal meetings of managers on an equivalent level are more likely, or more frequent, in a geographically centralized organization. Go to all these meetings with a genuine interest in listening to other managers difficulties and challenges. If you are following all the other edicts presented in this book, you will not be so uptight about your own world that your problems dominate your consciousness. There is a tendency, I know, for you to be occupied in such meetings with either your own points to be made, priorities to be stressed, or to be seething over the behavior of some other person ("that jerk in accounting," for example). Try very hard to get such preoccupying thoughts out of your mind. Be so well informed (do your homework!) that when your turn to make points comes, you can do so fluidly without having sat mentally practicing what you should say. Dismiss from your mind all negative thoughts about others in the room; they are highly destructive! Remember, that "Jerk" across the table is simply you, before you developed so much maturity! It is actually part of your job, now that you are mature, to help the "jerk" mature, for the benefit of the whole organization and you yourself.

Show a genuine interest in all participants in such meetings, and in what it is that they do. Incidentally, this is one of the several benefits of Japanese organizational practices. They stress cross-training all managers - with the result that most managers have genuine empathy for all others. Not so easy in the typical American system of fast and vertical promotions. But in the absence of a formal cross-training system, the mature manager must achieve the equivalent results.

In addition to the gradual increase in mutual support which comes with this approach, there is another important outcome. You will be seen as a mediator and as someone with broad interests beyond the parochial. Guess what kind of people organizations promote to high ranking and general management? Certainly not those who have been narrow in their interests. The only setting in which more independent managers are rewarded is one which is substantially immature; not a good place to be if you are mature yourself. . . and not a good place to be as the world matures.

In the case of a scattered, or geographically decentralized, organization the two advantages mentioned above are not so likely to exist. For this reason, you must be even more alert to your opportunities to build bridges. Whenever there are meetings which bring managers into face-to-face contact, it is even more imperative that you behave as recommended in No. 2, above. It will be a long time before the next chance, so don't blow it! Also, take the time to be more fully armed with some special information:

1) Anything new or significant which has gone on in someone else's bailiwick since your last contact with them. This could be directly related to your own activities, or not, in either case your knowing gives you an edge in fully understanding the current realities facing that other manager. If you are to have a chance in eliciting his/her support or even interest in your problems, this is but a simple and vital first step.

2) Major personal items, so-and-so has been ill, good old what's-her-name won some money in the lottery, etc. This trivia, and more importantly, the characteristics it displays just in the knowing of it, are the only substitutes you have for playing softball together (or whatever other social and informal contacts people have when they work in the same physical location.

3) Major crises and challenges being faced in the "other" area of responsibility.

Obviously, you cannot use so much time or resources in pursuit of these kinds of information that you fail to remain current in your own area, but it is very critical. Your ability to provide help and/or to help others in the larger decentralized group understand the needs of the afflicted is directly dependent on your efforts. Make this effort all the time!

One important note here. This "model" of altruistic management is directly contradictory to immature and "get yours" behaviors. In highly immature settings, you will be swimming upstream and occasionally getting "taken" when you use these approaches. This is all part of the price of progress. If you persist, and you must, rewards will be returned to you, ever so slowly at first, but ultimately the whole organization will improve and so will your own lot.

The ways in which size and structural characteristics, other than the degree of physical centralization, affect these behaviors must now be discussed.

INFORMALITY versus FORMALITY

Generally speaking, large organizations tend to be more formal in their cultural characteristics. In such settings, an individual may be able to deviate from the dominant cultural norms of behavior but only so much and in only so many ways. Again, as with the highly decentralized organization there are built-in difficulties not evident in the less formal firm. This means three things for you:

1) Doing the things necessary to comply with edict number 3 is a lot more difficult and often misunderstood.

2) It is even more important that you do strive for compliance with edict number 3.

3) It will take much longer to get results.

Part of the reason your efforts to behave maturely in a stiff and formal organization may falter is that the dominant behaviors of the mature are <u>informal</u> behaviors.   There is a greater tendency, in the formal organization and on the part of everyone therein, to use memo's for communications, and other <u>distancing</u> approaches (see Chapter 5 for specific communications guidelines).   The trappings of "office" are more in evidence and tend to delineate people and divide them and people "in office" tend to use their positional power more (see below).

Maturity and extreme formality are not mutually exclusive, but they are rarely found together.   If you find yourself in a very formal organization and no real maturity is being exhibited, you need to ask yourself the serious question: "Do I really belong here?"   There are some people who thrive in such environments, but I must say that the chances of applying, successfully, many of the edicts of this manual are relatively low.

THEORY

Another word for "formality," as it pertains to organizations, is BUREAUCRACY. Now I fully realize that this word connotes many negative things and can mean something quite narrow... but there is a comprehensive theory of bureaucracy and there are advantages to bureaucracy which I will discuss.

About the time of the First World War, a German intellectual by the name of Max Weber was writing passionately about the wrongs of feudal power and authority which had dominated European governments and social systems on every level. His concern was largely centered in the reality that social justice was thwarted and thus, the opportunity to be recognized based on individual qualifications negated. His concern for the individual rights, however, were not so profound as his conviction that a legitimate placement of power in the organization, based on merit, would produce much higher levels of efficiency. His attempt to build theory in the form of a "pure" type bureaucracy has had heavy impact on the study of organizations and indeed their evolution.

Weber envisioned organizations in which nepotism, in all its forms, would be eliminated, office-holders would all meet some prescribed competencies, and promotions would be based entirely on merit. He declared that the devices to ensure such ideals would be the very precise files and records of the organization (ensuring absolute consistency and adherence to rules and policies) and very clearly described and limited authority for every position.

In the real world of today's organizational setting, job descriptions, files, policies and power limitations are to be found everywhere. The degree to which these devices dictate absolute behaviors is the measure of bureaucracy and formality. In less formal organizations there is much more flexibility, but what about efficiency? What are the variables which might tend to "tighten" an organization, or make it more formal? Three things:

1) The degree of uncertainty felt by senior and middle managers.

2) Success levels; goals being met, or not.

3) The degree to which the top management (individuals, or a small cadre) involve middle managers and others in the planning and other decisions.

The significance of these factors should unfold in the following sections.

SIZE AS A FACTOR

The larger an organization, the less likely it is that top management really knows "what is actually going on." This is a reality which forces many key executives to hold tight the reins and limit the authority of people in lower management positions. Exacerbating variables are:

1) The turbulence of the industry (in a slow-to-change environment, certainty is less than in a slowly changing situation).

2) The MATURITY of the people in subordinate roles, and of the senior managers. My notion of Maturity does not necessarily equate with age, success or experience!

3) Economic rise and fall. When times are good, people tend to relax a little, and to become very tense when the marketplace is tough.   It should be readily apparent that the larger an organization, the more likely that there are structural divisions and other complications.   Therefore, characteristics of centralization and/or formal or bureaucratic organization should be considered probable concomitants of large size.

On the last point, Larry Greiner (1972) proposed that as organizations grow, they go through various phases propelled by different "forces." In the first phase organizational growth is driven by the entrepreneurial spirit of the founder(s), but this ends in a crisis of bad management (these terms are mine, not Greiner's).   The solution (phase two) is "Professional Management" and delegation, but this, ultimately leads to a crisis of control - to which the answer (all too often) is the third phase of bureaucracy or formality and the imposition of policies and other restrictions.   The trade-off for the realized control, of course, is inflexibility and red tape.   There are other phases in the Greiner model, but you get the picture.   Coincidentally, Greiner envisioned collaboration as the ultimate positive phase; to me collaboration and acknowledged interdependency seem to be the same things!

The materials in the section which follows, on organizational culture, also have major connections to size, as you will see.

THE DOMINANT POWER CULTURE

While there are many aspects of organizations and ways in which we might examine their "cultures," none is more important than the "Power Culture." This simply means the normal patterns of power distribution throughout the organization: who wields power, of what sort, under what circumstances and why? Size is very significant in this, though size does not always predict, correctly, the power culture. In very small, entrepreneurial, firms, power is often centered in one individual: the owner/founder. But even this can vary, some entrepreneurial individuals being less dominant than others. To generalize, in highly technical or scientific entrepreneurial endeavors it is more likely that the founder/owner is content to delegate power and decision-making than in a situation with less technical/scientific products; but this is a bit of an unfair generalization.

Don't forget that bureaucracy, as an organizational dimension, dictates a kind of formal, or constrained decentralization and distribution of power, and thus also constrains flexibility. In order for you to function effectively as a mature manager, there must be a match-up between your self perceived ability and maturity and your freedom to act, your autonomy. A mismatch, either too much freedom to act, or too little, inevitably leads to your frustration and will slow your continuing growth.

One of the problems with job interviewing (see Chapter 6) is that the real organizational issues, such as this one, rarely get discussed openly. Yet, the degree to which you can be free to make or influence decisions, and the relative significance of those decisions, and how these variables "fit" your preparation and readiness, are the key factors in how well you do your job; and in how you feel about your work. This critical match-up is also true for all the people under your influence. Not only will your frustration level be painfully evident to you, but your colleagues will also feel and see it, though they may well misinterpret the behaviors exhibited.

SOURCES OF POWER

Power is defined as the ABILITY to influence others, Authority, on the other hand, is the designated RIGHT to apply influence. Extending these fundamentals, we find that power and authority come from (in most cases) different sources, and that there are different kinds of Power.

Personal Power

This, sometimes referred to as Charisma, was seen by Max Weber as an illegitimate form of power, having no place in a bureaucracy. Today, with the world operating in quite a different manner from Germany at the turn of the century, we accept that some people, by their personality and other personal characteristics, are indeed more influential than others. But, in highly bureaucratic or formal organizations, this particular source of power is not especially significant. In more informal settings individual and personal traits play a significant part in determining who has the influence. Remember, none of these sources of power is self-sufficient or omnipotent. Also, the mature manager is well aware of the "right" time to exert influence from each of the power bases.

Expert and Referent Power

"Knowledge is Power," as the saying goes. Certainly this can be the case, however the knowledge in question must have some significance and relevance for the situation at hand. Technical expertise in a non-technical situation, or where the dominant variables are non-technical, will not buy the expert much influence. The problem, or at least a major influencing variable, is that as one rises through the ranks of management in a complex organization, the further removed one becomes from the technicalities. An immature manager may, to compensate for his/her perception of "lost" expert power, attempt to substitute or exert influence from another power base. . . most often that of the "position." This tends to elevate perceptions of bureaucracy and frustrates the people in follower positions. Rapidly changing technology brings about changes in locus of power. In the mature, such shifts are not threatening but for the immature exists an imperative to substitute one form of power for another. Usually this means an elevation in bureaucracy.

Positional Power

This, in essence, is the same thing as authority. It is "legitimate" (in Weber's view) and tends to be well understood by all in the organization. Actually, in some very complex organizations it may be quite confusing. In the military, this confusion is eliminated by designations of rank; everyone knows that a Major outranks a Captain in the army, for instance. And all must wear, in two or three highly visible areas, the signs of rank! But in organizations of great complexity the ones with the power are not wearing rank insignia; too often the relative positional power across departmental or divisional lines is confused.

There is nothing wrong with asserting one's positional power, but there is an old saying, "those with real power never have to prove it!" The organizational threats which come with position (withholding rewards and administering punishments) are very discouraging for those without power from some other base. This means that positional power must be used very sparingly indeed. In situations where you need to inculcate openness and trust, it is inadvisable to use positional power. Everyone involved knows the realities of rank. Instead, use any personal or expert power you may have, but do not "exert" it. By contrast, if you have tried to have an errant employee commit to the organization, without success, and you have tried everything else, then your positional power, with all its available rewards and threats, may be a last resort.

You should know, also, that the tendency exists, within us all, to hold on to our power or substitute positional power for that which is lost or in other ways not available. You must resist this temptation. In the final analysis, your ability to influence will be undermined or destroyed if you use positional power when it is not needed.

In the organizational setting there are "trappings" of office which can also be abusive. I refer to the "architecture" of your office, such as the desk, your diploma's and other signs of your legitimacy. Use these things very carefully. If you do not need a college diploma on the wall (for a physician it might be justifiable) then keep them in the closet. When you have a subordinate in your office, sit on the same side of the desk they do.... there is no need to amplify your positional power; or better yet, meet very often on neutral ground, or on "their" turf. These tactics will enhance your personal power and, at the same time, allow the employees to hold onto all their sources of power. When negotiating with anyone, hold back on the power trappings until you really need them. Remember, it is your responsibility to enhance the maturation of all your people; the maturity you display in not using your position heavy-handedly will maximize potentials in this respect. It is adherence to the values inherent in this which makes for high quality work environments such as that at Hewlett-Packard and others of the same caliber.

True communications and the relationships which are engendered, can only develop when power differentials are minimized. Incidentally, there are several other sources of power, such as Money... your employees know that resource decisions are in your hands, minimize the resentment by encouraging their participation in decisions about resource allocation. Do not make the mistake of "assigning" their budgets to them, make it at least a shared analysis. Encourage their growth and their maturation along with your own. Power, to be meaningful, is a shared trust!

Even in the practice of Law our courts have acted to protect those (even those in breach of a contract) when it is shown that there is significant disparity between contracting parties' power in forming the contract. In fact, the courts refer to such contracts as "unconscionable." It is often difficult to show such disparity, but managers often forget the various ways in which such disparities are amplified by their own behaviors and the trappings they use.

Chronic and persistent perceptions of significant power differences, at least those involving mismatch between one's own abilities and the concomitant autonomy, result in frustration, one of the most discouraging of emotions and one which assures slow or no growth for those frustrated. It is true that some personality types deal with frustration better than others; it is also true that some levels of frustration act as motivators for some people. Positive motivators, however are far more effective.

THEORY: The Topic of Frustration

Frustration is a condition which results from real or perceived and relative powerlessness. It is inevitable that we all feel it sometimes and it is not always bad. It is the choices (sometimes unconscious) we make in dealing with frustration which can be "bad." Bad for us in terms of our own health or bad for us in terms of the external effects, on others, for example.

Some Behavioral Outcomes of Frustration

Aggression

Overt and negative behaviors which tend to alienate and separate people. Since interdependency cannot thrive in such circumstances, this frustration outcome must be avoided or maturation is virtually unattainable.

Repression

The inward direction of negative energies and the pretense, on the part of the repressor, that all is well. Unfortunately, the unconscious mind knows the real state of affairs and prevents those who repress their frustrations from approaching others (especially those who might be the source of the frustration) with real openness. There may be phony openness, but this has no real foundation and is often seen by others in the system as "obvious kissing up." The result of this would be rejection by almost everyone in the whole system, except other repressors, perhaps.

Diversion

The tendency to allow frustrations to create major energy flows away from the source of the frustration. This can be a healthy way of dealing with the situation for the employee affected, but inevitably results in high energy commitments away from the job.

Acquiescence

This is a kind of internal acknowledgement that the system must be right, that "I," the frustrated, am not worthwhile or that there is really no point in trying to elevate oneself. There is a lot of rationalizing attendant with this response and obviously this will not foster maturity.

Resignation

This is an extreme form of acquiescence and can result in high absenteeism, tardiness and very real physical health problems. Mature managers are not likely to induce these conditions in others or to respond in any of these ways themselves. However, there is no such thing as absolute maturity and any one of us can be partially blind to the evidence of these signs, in ourselves and in others, especially if they are sporadic or at low levels. We must be constantly on the look out for them however, or the manifestation of their existence will be some shortfall performance of our team.

PRODUCT HOMOGENEITY and Structural Interdependency

The meaning of maturity in an organization is having system-wide appreciation for outcomes of decisions and actions. In an organization where there is considerable homogeneity of effort, there is also greater likelihood of genuine understanding and appreciation of individual contributions. By contrast, in a setting where everyone is doing something different (heterogeneity) there is great potential for misunderstanding. This, as previously discussed, is the basis of all cultural clashes. It is also, ironically, the setting in which greater maturity is called for but least likely.

As James Thompson first pointed out (1960) there is also a great deal of latent conflict associated with individual and personal attributes. He identified age, education, cultural background, etc., as personal differences laden with potential for non-communications and non-collaboration. I contend that efforts to build maturity can overcome most of these latencies and, indeed, those which are structurally induced. You will find further reference to these specifics in later chapters.

Make sure that YOU come to terms with the level of homogeneity within your organization's products, services and processes so that you can be on your guard against the cultural clashes which come up. Also, at every opportunity, make certain that others in the organization slowly come to understand these latent disputes. Remember though, the problems do not always surface. More often, there is a whole lot of behavior on the part of participants everywhere which reflect their own frustration levels, resulting in poor performances, or failure to rise to the highest levels of maturity and productivity. The frustrated workers do not always know they are frustrated... they often do not know that they aren't productive. They only have a vague feeling of dissatisfaction and they look forward to Friday night. What you need to inculcate is an excitement about Monday mornings. You must have a growing perception on the part of most employees, that work is an exciting and challenging experience which provides them with challenges matching their self-perceptions of competence.

The workplace must be where people feel significant as individuals, but more importantly as a part of a team. From your position and using mature approaches, you can help ensure that kind of progression for yourself, your employees and your colleagues. The role of mature communications have a special significance in this process, as you will discover in the next chapter.

Chapter Four, I know, has been substantially theoretical. This was necessary, at this stage, so that the two very applied and practical chapters that follow can be understood more fully. I hope you agree.

CHAPTER 5

Mature Communications

MEMO'S, EDICTS, MEETINGS,
and Other Immaturity Traps

MEMORANDA & LETTERS

One of the highly visible ways in which people display their immaturity is in their several ways of attempting communication. It is vital that mature managers remember that communication exists in the mind of the receiver, nowhere else! As I write these words, I am struggling to choose concepts and ideas which have potential significance for readers. There is an old business axiom in which I used to place great faith: Don't tell it, write it! At this stage of my life, I have come full circle, however. I would now urge you to heed . . .

EDICT No. 4:   DON'T WRITE IT, UNLESS YOU
                     REALLY MUST!

One of the many problems with written communication is that there is often a powerful unstated message, or, as Marshall McLuhan sees it, "The Medium is The Message." What McLuhan is trying to say, I believe, is that our choice of media sometimes communicates more, and often a different message, than the intended message itself. Let me illustrate. You would not, I hope, write a memorandum to your son or daughter to communicate your appreciation for something accomplished, or to comment on a failure. And why not? Well, for one thing, it is too impersonal; for another, it eliminates the possibility of two-way exchange (except for another wrong choice of a memo back). It prevents amplification of message and feeling which can come from non-verbal communication (details in a moment) and it is also far too ponderous and delayed a communication type for the message involved. The unstated message is, or could be, "I'm too embarrassed, or too busy, or too something to really communicate with you, so I'll write you!" Now, obviously, absence or physical separation (such as that between you and me) is a complication which may change the edict, and could justify the writing, but there is still only partial communication. A great deal of what would be really communicated in a face-to-face exchange is missing. I am talking, of course about non-verbal devices (sometimes incompletely labeled "body language"). The inflection of voice, the facial expressions, the incredibly communicative eyes as well as bodily posture, choice of venue, timing and setting can all amplify or at least modify a communicative attempt. As rich as our language may be, it is inadequate!

When you choose to write someone (who is in daily or reasonably frequent contact) you are conveying a message quite apart from the one constructed on the paper. You are also missing the opportunity to really communicate (two-way) and to enhance the potential for real understanding beyond the immediate. So many managers, and others, make this dreadful mistake and in so doing convey information which is not necessarily valid and, worse, establish a far too formal basis for the relationship which does not facilitate genuine understanding and does not open doors for really intense communication to take place. It establishes a formality, in other words, and thus presages all other aspects of the relationship.

Should one NEVER write memo's? Of course memo's have their place and value, especially in the following circumstances.

1) When facts are to be on record for future or continuing reference.

2) As a follow-up, punctuation, clarification of previously communicated information; AND when personal non-written methods are inconvenient, impossible or disruptive.

3) When what has to be communicated is complex or lengthy, but

only then with explicit understanding that there are open channels or dialogue and discussion.

EDICT No. 5:   NEVER WRITE A MEMO OR LETTER SIMPLY TO CYA!

If you find yourself writing something with the idea that you need to "cover" some part of your anatomy in some way, you are either extremely immature or you're surrounded by immaturity, or both. If the memorandum delivers an EDICT, you are in even more trouble! Make sure that all edicts, if they are really necessary, are well communicated IN PERSON before anyone sees them in writing. This means a lot of hard work on the part of yourself and everyone else, but, I repeat, NO EDICT SHOULD EVER COME AS A SURPRISE! Preferably, of course, all tough and distasteful decisions, especially those which impinge on worker sovereignty or in other ways frustrate, should be made only after considerable discussion and debate. . . then as a kind of reluctant choice on your part. As I said in Chapter One, workers will tolerate some heavy-handedness on your part; but the key is that it should be seen as a deviance from your usual personal method and as an isolated, infrequent and anomalous necessity.

Letter-writing is, of course, a little different from internal memo's and is more tolerable, even desirable. The external interfaces section (Chapter Eight) deals with some of this, but let's consider for a moment the possibility of letter-writing between departments or individuals in the same organization.

The difference between a letter and a memorandum, chiefly, is that the letter is always more formal in some specific ways. It usually is formally, rather than informally addressed. It is also more formally closed, with rather specific rules of salutation, etc. For these reasons alone, it is automatically more distancing even than the memo. Of course, the tone of any written document is a modifier and so the selection of appropriate mood and tone, in writing anything, is critical. But no smoothing incurred by soft tones can eradicate the formality of any letter or memo. The choice of the medium and method, then is the first critical decision. It might be good at this juncture to provide an example which illustrates my points.

Let's say you are a sales executive and you have made a decision on a special case involving one of your employees. It is a negative decision on appeal for consideration of extenuating circumstances to allow a field representative to receive partial commission on the sale of goods to a large customer with multiple locations. Lets say that company policy is to pay commissions only to representatives with customer head offices in their territories and on their routine call list. The appeal in this case is based on the fact that a sub-location of the customer had, until a few months ago, been independent but was recently acquired by the larger firm. "We" had never done business with the acquired firm before the acquisition, but the sales representative in that area had been calling regularly and had done much groundwork, had made some progress. Ignoring, for the moment, the question of whether or not the negative decision is correct, your challenge is to communicate to all interested parties the decision. You have used personal interviews in obtaining the facts and input from everyone, now choose the media and methods to close the issue.

Consider Two Options:

1) Writing a memo to the appellant sales representative with a copy to the sales representative who is the recipient of the commission on the account. Include both the decision and the rationale as well as appropriate H.R. remarks which acknowledge the appellant and his/her efforts. Use a tone that is humanistic yet firm. Advise all other representatives, in writing, of the ruling, for future reference, and the rationale. Write, also, to senior officers regarding other divisions of the firm and the advisability of a common corporate policy interpretation. (Actually, such communication should, some would argue, have been part of the fact-finding activity before making the decision!)

2) Doing all of the above but using personal or telephone contacts with the main actors, the directly affected representatives. But advising the non-personally involved and the file system with memoranda.

   There are, of course other options and variations on each of these alternatives, but let's consider the pro's and con's of the main aspects of each of these two. You'll notice I ruled out the letter form in any aspect of this particular communicative attempt. I believe the very personal nature of the problem and the criticality of the decision and its impact on individuals eliminate not only the letter format but also the memorandum for all but those on the sidelines. For those directly involved, the two sales representatives, you MUST be fully in engagement with them to properly communicate this decision. Not only the appellant, for all the obvious reasons, but also the beneficiary. You see, off the official record, you may want to "suggest" that the latter make personal reparations with the appellant, maybe even a voluntary gift or other sharing gesture, if he/she does not think of it themselves. Such "recommendations" must be handled very delicately AND with yourself literally "out of role."

All very personal decisions should indeed be communicated on a colleagial basis, rather than bureaucratically. The telephone CAN be used if, and only if, you are spatially separated from the communicants and will not be in face-to-face contact with them in the very near future. Or if you cannot get into face-to-face contact relatively easily or at low cost. When such conditions prevail, you must preface your remarks with a comment that you would much prefer to communicate personally on the issue. The urgency of the decision, you must say, and the time lost before a next contact, make necessary this inferior method of communicating. ACKNOWLEDGE IT!

Alternative No. 2 then is far superior. Those people "on the sidelines" are not sufficiently and currently involved for the written communication to fail (assuming appropriate words are chosen). The decision in this case is made imperative by the very personal nature of the outcome; personal earnings are at stake, and there is a "winner" and a "loser." In other words, the extreme (and rather obvious) impact of the decision on individuals helps us understand the ways in which (and which not) to communicate. It is very natural for us to use such considerations in making the decision, less natural, perhaps, for us to use these same factors in communicating with all parties concerned. This particular example also has some other aspects which make it a good learning model. The people on the sidelines (other sales representatives, maybe the payroll people) are NOT directly affected by this particular decision, but can be affected by the long term implications. Having them come to fully comprehend the rules of the game is a major part of your responsibility as a manager. There is a third and very important factor...of all attributes you need to faithfully eschew, consistency is perhaps the most important; but fairness and tough-mindedness are equally critical. The processes you use in reaching your decisions and of communicating them to all people in your organization are key indicators of your own maturity and, significantly, are tremendously influential in helping (or hindering, if bungled) the maturation of your people and thus, the whole organizational unit.

MEETINGS

On the subject of meetings I'll start with an edict:

EDICT No 6:   MEETINGS YOU CALL ARE NOT "YOUR" OWN MEETINGS

Formal group/department meetings, I find, are so badly abused and in so many ways. With the tremendous expansion of meetings, in number and declared purposes, this places all organizations at great risk of losing much ground on the maturity issue. There is tremendous potential for this loss of ground in poorly conceived and conducted meetings, don't fall into one or more of the following "great meeting traps."

Meeting Trap Number One

You find that a small number of individuals are failing or falling-short in some specific way or ways. You call a meeting to reacquaint everyone with the desired behavior or outcomes, or worse, to read the riot act. The problem with this is that since most individuals are not out of conformity, they feel denigrated by the lengthy treatment of the subject in question and the apparent attempt to tar everyone with the same brush. Worse yet, many of those who are in conformity know exactly who is not and they resent the fact that valuable time is being spent "in group."

These same people are also likely to conclude that either you are not fully aware who is and who is not a transgressor OR that you haven't the guts to deal with offenders one-on-one! Either way, you lose by proving to everyone your own immaturity and by treating everyone as though they were also immature. You also waste a good deal of everyone's time, including your own. Of course, if everyone is out of compliance in the same way, communicating with all involved in the same meeting can be efficient so long as it is done in mature ways. The real question you must ask if everyone is out of step, is "just how effective a communicator are YOU?"

When you do have deviant performance by one or a few, in any respect, instead of calling meetings to "correct" the situation, do the following four Mature things:

1) Acknowledge those who are performing to or above standards.

2) In subtle ways let everyone know that you are aware of the non-performers.

3) Consult the best performers for suggestions on methods they use and their suggestions on how to deal with offenders. Do not disclose non-performer identity or specific parameters which might indicate identity.

4) Confront non-performers individually, privately, consistently, calmly and set meaningful goals and time-tables for reevaluation. (See also Chapter 6)

5) Follow-up on your plans and time-tables, take firm action if standards for progress have not been met. Acknowledge, warmly, appropriate progress (see the former section on communications).

Meeting Trap Number Two

You have a regularly scheduled meeting, the same day of each week, or month, for example. You "find" agenda items to ensure that the meeting time is filled.

The problem here is that it is always possible to fill available meeting time; but more important there is the lost time AND especially the erosion of commitment which otherwise comes when everyone leaves each meeting feeling that they really "got" something of value. If people get the sense that you are really groping for issues to fill available time, they lose faith in your leadership, they become convinced that you hold meetings merely to hear the sound of your own voice, they allow their own immaturity to dominate their feelings and behaviors (with such things as criticism, back-biting or gossip).

On the subject of gossip, let's digress a little and think about this subject in connection with something discussed in Chapter Four of this book, powerlessness and resultant frustration. Gossip, at least that which occurs in organizations, is often a manifestation of powerlessness, or more properly stated, of the frustration which comes from a sense of powerlessness. Those people who feel left out, or not informed, if they are immature, "invent" their own information. Those readers who have served in the military know quite well that military life is a place where gossip and rumor spreading are rampant. When military action is at high potential, but still pending and uncertain, rumor-mongering hits a peak. This is explainable by the fact that there is a human tendency to "invent" information to improve one's own image or to give us a (false) sense of power. Nervous tension which comes from accompanying uncertainty and related to threats to personal safety exacerbates the problem producing even higher levels of misinformation. It is a curious phenomenon of human nature that those with real power never have to use it; the powerless, it seems, unless they are completely withdrawn or resigned to their fate, must find a way to use power they do not really have.

The tendency to "fill" available meeting time (and indeed, the slavish notion that meetings are a good way to communicate with people generally) should be resisted in the name of maturity and good sense. But the meeting can be of immense value (any meeting) if the following conditions are met:

1) There is a reason for meeting which everyone understands ahead of time. By the way, it is also very immature, unless you have a real Machiavellian reason, to call a meeting without letting everyone know the purposes, their individual role and the agenda.

2) There is strict adherence to the planned agenda, even if the plan is to hold a substantially unstructured meeting.

3) Everyone has a definite need to be involved (in some cases this needs to be carefully communicated before the meeting takes place).

4) Some form of closure, on every topic, is very well understood by everyone in attendance. This calls for you, or someone designated as responsible, to articulate a close and make sure that everyone

has had ample opportunity for their input and to understand what happens next on the issue in question. This may mean simply agreeing that the matter be tabled, or that more information is needed. Regardless, for each topic be sure that these understandings are universally held and that those with responsibility for any type of follow-up acknowledge such responsibility clearly.

5) There is a democratic process during the meeting and everyone is treated even-handedly and with dignity. A little light "kidding" of selected individuals is permissible, but make certain you only "kid" the relatively mature. To take the risk of embarrassing an immature or uncertain individual, is itself immature.

6) You follow-up every "dangling" item personally, either providing answers/actions promised or asking everyone with follow-up responsibility if you can help them fulfill their assignment.

7) You start with the acknowledgement that all those in attendance at the meeting are expected to contribute and share responsibility for the advancement of understanding of something very specific and important.

IN OTHER WORDS, IN A SUCCESSFUL MEETING, EVERYONE'S NEEDS MUST BE MET, NOT JUST YOURS! And this is also true in the special case of the formal or informal one-on-one meeting; which calls for the next edict.

EDICT No. 7:   BE CAREFUL ABOUT ALLOCATING YOUR
                      TIME TO OTHERS.

The key item here is not so much WHAT you do as it is with WHOM! Let's take your lunch time companions, for example. There is a great temptation, I know, to spend your lunch times, and other informal time with those individuals in your organization for whom you have affinity. These people, normally, will be the "winners" in your organization and they will be the most mature. The problem is in the perceptions of the less mature, the ones with whom you seldom spend precious time. Immaturity will bring them to all kinds of selfish and errant conclusions about the relationship you have with your most frequent lunch-time companions. Oddly, most of us would fully understand the "wrong conclusions" being reached if your favorite lunch partner is of the opposite sex. It is exactly this same kind of impression, though not sexually oriented, which you must also avoid. Not only is this wise for the reasons identified, but there is an even more compelling reason: the less mature people can benefit most, and thus grow themselves, from more opportunities to rub shoulders with you. This is not merely political, but is directly related to your most important role as mentor. The more mature persons in your department need less contact with, and influence from, you AND are less likely to feel some of the many forms of exclusion and jealousy felt by the less mature.

This same kind of logic applies especially to your allocation of formal time to people. So, as an exercise designed to improve your performance in this, record, for a week or two, time spent with all the different individuals coming under your supervision, identify who initiated the contact in each case. Identify, using the criteria previously spelled out, people of Low, Intermediate and High levels of maturity. Determine the breakdown of time spent with people in each at each level of maturity, on a per-person basis, and a per group basis. You should be spending most time (per-person) with the less mature, though the amount of time per-group will depend on the numbers in each group. Of course, special circumstances, such as a special assignment or crisis, would modify this edict, but in the normal course of events, apply . . .

EDICT No. 8:   GIVE MORE TIME TO THOSE WHO NEED YOUR INFLUENCE MOST!
(those who are least mature themselves)

and the corollary:

EDICT No. 9:   SPEND LESS TIME WITH YOUR MOST MATURE EMPLOYEES!

There are cynics who suggest that the very immature cannot be "salvaged," and in some cases I agree (See Chapter 9), but among the very immature there is at least potential for significant growth. The old saying "a chain is only as strong as its weakest link," at least in part, applies here. Your organization is led by the strongest people, but it is hampered by the weakest. For these reasons, and the obvious other reason of perceptions by those lowest on the totem pole, major blocks of time spent with the strongest people in your unit represents immaturity on YOUR part. This is especially true, also, of informal time and semi-formal time. Examine the patterns you recorded with these thoughts in mind. Change what needs to be changed!

I'll close this very applied section on another topic which is relevant in many organizations: Slogans, Posters, etc., then I'll end the chapter with some theoretical discussions.

SLOGANS AND POSTERS

Slogans, motto's, acronyms, or other contrivances which are designed and used in the hope that they will build enthusiasm and commitment are really based on an assumption of immaturity. Mature people treated in mature ways find their own ways of building their fires of enthusiasm without such trivialities. Not only that, but as forms of communication they are incomplete and invite reductionism, or focusing on the "fun" of the item itself, instead of on the objectives envisioned.

I once worked in a very large manufacturing organization, many thousands of employees in different divisions, highly diversified products and geographically decentralized. At one point, the President came up with the slogan "Commitment to Quality." There is nothing wrong with the sentiment behind the idea of quality, and, in a large organization there are many immature people who do not see or comprehend the "mission" and goals of the organization. But unless there is dynamic change of organizational processes, unless the majority of workers, at every level and in every function, feel responsible for quality and a strong desire to contribute to the maximum of their ability, then the slogan will do virtually nothing. They must, of course INTERNALIZE these and all objectives, not merely be informed about and understand them. In fact, there is danger that the introduction of a slogan without PRIOR INTERNALIZATION, the use of slogans and their imposition on workers, can become rancorous, derisive.

At Motorola, for the last several years, there has been a serious (and successful) attempt to build quality into all products at the time of design and manufacture. Their failure rate (products in the field) has dropped to such a low percentage as to be virtually zero. Motorola talks of this success as SIX SIGMA, and employees at every level take pride in the accomplishments represented. Six Sigma relates to the left and right tails of the normal distribution curve. Those familiar with statistics know that 99.97% of all "events" fall within six standard deviations ($+/-$ 3) of the mean. This means that Motorola shoots for, and by all accounts comes close to attaining, a failure rate of 3 in 10,000! The point is that the performance communicates more than the slogan, especially in this case because many people, perhaps most, do not understand the precise meaning of the slogan.

At IBM, where a long history of success has built an assumption that they are always doing the right thing, the slogan "THINK" is used extensively. Current difficulties for the computer giant have stimulated some creative thinking of the sort not planned. Wags within have been tempted to add the words "OR THWIM" to the slogan. Remember, this is a place where terminations are referred to as "Management Initiated Attrition!" Any bureaucracy indicated here?

Posters on the wall, acronyms which spell out someone's pet program, fancy words on the bottom of the letterhead, little gimmicky awards and celebrations are, in and of themselves, attempts to communicate which cannot communicate very well UNLESS all other forms of communications are clicking, and are mature. Consider, in a personal relationship, the wonderful words "I Love You." If your behavior communicates something different from love, then expressing your love in words is not very persuasive. So it is with sayings however cleverly dressed up!

In Chapter Six, dealing with Hiring, Evaluating, etc., there is obviously much more on this vital subject of communications, but for those interested in examining some theoretical aspects of the subject, the following few pages of academics are offered. . . skip to Chapter Six at this point if you wish.

COMMUNICATIONS THEORY

As noted at the beginning of this chapter, communications guru Marshall McLuhan once said, "The Medium IS the Message (emphasis mine). What he meant, of course, is that media has the capability of communicating something quite apart from the intended message, sometimes that "something" is so powerful that the intended message never gets through.

It is important to start this theoretical section with the assertion that communication takes place in the mind of the receiver. Whatever the receiver "gets" is what is communicated. This is why body language and architecture are so important in business communications and also personal communications.

Non-Verbal Language

Body Language, in its simplest form, includes facial expression, bodily posture, etc. which communicates something to anyone watching. A frown, a smile, pursing of lips and eyebrow raising, all very interesting aspects of human behavior, all capable of amplifying or belying the words and expressions being used by a speaker. But there is so much more to it than this, hence the more inclusive term Non-Verbal Language.

It is a valid assumption about humans that there is no such state or condition as "Non-Behavior." Everyone who is alive is doing something all the time. Admittedly, some behaviors are more passive, some more active. Some also are more Expressive, some more easily interpreted. But good communicators learn that every nuance of their behavior can add to, or detract from, the communications possibilities.

Mark Knapp (1972) identified six specific ways in which non-verbal behaviors affect the "message" and what is communicated. These, of course, are entirely capable of acting on communicative efforts in concert; making the whole issue very complicated and subject to a lot of interference (noise) and in other ways producing unpredictable outcomes.

1) Non-verbal behaviors may repeat what is expressed verbally.

2) Non-verbal behaviors may contradict verbal expression.

3) Non-verbal behaviors may substitute for what could be expressed.

4) Non-verbal behaviors may modify what is expressed verbally.

5) Non-verbal behaviors may emphasize components of expression.

6) The flow of verbal expression may be regulated by nonverbal behaviors. For example, if a receiver is fidgety the deliverer of the message may cut short, or slow down, the delivery, or in other ways modify what is said.

Note, on this last point, and it is true for most of the others, the behaviors of the receiver play a part. All behavior has the potential for being a stimulus to behaviors in others in any setting. Behavior, then, is both a stimulus and a response. This makes the communications equation very complex indeed.

Architecture

The voluntary and involuntary gestures and expressions of people in their attempts to communicate are only part of the non-verbal communications challenge. Items other than the body itself can have some of the same potentials for interference or amplification. In communications theory we talk of noise and, as in radio transmission, anything which is carried along with the signal, or more precisely, anything unintended which is received along with the signal, is NOISE. If you are a salesperson and you wear a very flashy item of jewelry, or clothing, or if you have an unusual haircut, etc., you are risking that these items introduce noise in your communications. That is, the distractions induced literally lower the threshold of perception for your verbal and other non-verbal behaviors.

The location chosen for communication is also potentially critical. If your office is formal, your desk is large, and you sit behind that desk, guess what? It is virtually impossible to communicate in a less formal or friendly vein. Neutral turf, on the other hand, is a place where there is neither enhancement of the power/formality of the sender or of the message. Much of the environment of communications has potential for these effects.

Figure 2 A Communications Model

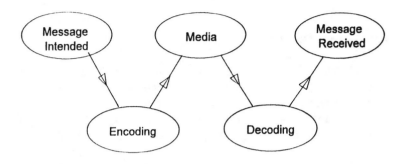

As you can see from the above depiction of One-Way communications, there are several complex steps in the process; each step having its own challenges and difficulties.

Intended Message

It would be very nice if everyone who wished to communicate something actually knew exactly what they wanted others to understand, but such is not always the case. All too often the message is constructed without prior attention to this critical phase. What you want to say is not necessarily based on what you want understood. In case you do not follow the significance of the gap here, let's assume you are in a crowded theater and you see evidence of fire. What do you want to communicate? Is it that there is fire or is it that there is good reason for evacuation? The problem is that if you stood up and shouted, loudly, "there is good reason for evacuation," the response may not be suitable.

On the other hand, shouting "Fire" may produce panic and stampede. Every situation involving formal communications calls for similar analysis of not only what it is you want understood, but also what responses you desire.

There is the classic story of the CEO, on the golf course with two Vice-Presidents. Said the CEO, "I wonder if we would really lose much if we closed down the Dallas operation and covered that market out of Houston?" The next week, our CEO received a report that Dallas was closed as requested!

Encoding and Decoding

The choice of words seems such an innocuous thing, really, yet picture this. . . you are an accountant (I could have chosen a message from an engineer, sales representative, or whatever, all have their own peculiarities, or cultural differences. See Chapter 4 again.) and you choose to send a message using the words (code) which follows:

The assets held in subsidiary entities, having been acquired prior to the 1990 and 1991 mergers, have been depreciated differentially. In the case of ABC Company assets the straight-line method was used whereas XYZ used units of production. Since these methods are both different from the parent company method, we have no clear picture of a uniform costing method, all overhead factors considered. We also are in the dark with regard to current position on these assets, because in the acquisition agreements the specific value by asset item was not detailed.

What exactly is our accountant trying to convey? There is no doubt that he/she understands this, and many readers do too, but surely, the chosen code (words, phrases, etc.) should be chosen with the receiver in mind. To do otherwise is to ignore the realities of communications gaps. If someone does not speak your language,and you wish to communicate with them, then YOU must learn their language. This language difference can exist as an outcome of training, education (or lack of it) or experience - all elements of culture.

Media

As stated previously, the choice of medium is as critical as any other component in the communications attempt. The previous section (this chapter) on memoranda and letters should be reexamined with this communications model in mind. Media selection must be made with, again, the receiver, the mood, the climate, the conditions and the message clearly understood by the sender.

Other Communications Theories

The flow of formal information within any organization is dependent upon the channels created for the flow. The requirement for a flow, as with the flow of water down a river or stream, is dependent on the structural arrangement of channels and blockages. Harold Guetzkow suggested, nearly three decades ago, that information flows occur, depending on structural configurations, simultaneously or serially (parallel or serial).

Obviously, information which is transmitted from one person directly to another is an example of serial flow. But often information is disseminated to a group of people through memoranda, letters, internal newspapers, etc., this being simultaneous transmission. When a restricted group is fed information, collectively, and then each of those people passes on the information to individuals, there is a combination of transmission types at work. Timing is often a key factor in determining which flow systems to utilize, but often overlooked is the very necessary feed-back which is a requirement for feelings of involvement to develop, an important feature of Mature Management. The simultaneous method of communication is invariably limited in spontaneous and instantaneous feed-back and therefore excludes the advantages of Two-Way communications. The typical hierarchical arrangement of people and power in complex organizations virtually assure that most information flows from the top down. The problem is that in many situations, and for many types of information, information only available at the bottom is vital for senior management decision making. This is especially true of marketplace realities and of many problem areas in manufacturing. Healthy and mature organizations must ensure that information flows can be up, down and horizontal.

There are some interesting theoretical depictions of formal communications networks in the literature, and I direct the reader who wishes to expand on what is touched upon here to the reference materials in the back section (appendix) of this book.

Informal Communications

I have often claimed that information which is dammed, like a river, will find its way in spite of attempts to block it. The flow of water in a dammed river, unless there is a release or overflow built into the system, will destroy the dam or create a new waterway. So it is with information in an organization. The problem in the organization which is closed (dammed), however, is that human behavioral tendencies change the nature of what flows. Frustrated (powerless) people who are kept "in the dark" will modify information or invent new information in a quirky way of grasping power, or the perception of such. The more powerless people feel, the more inventive the rumor-mongering. There is perhaps nothing so rife with rumor as the military... a nearly perfect bureaucracy with formal badges of office, separation by ranks, nearly universal top-down arrangement for information flows AND a set of real reasons for NOT passing on information unless there is need to know.

Since information of one sort or another will flow, and since many informal channels will develop, it behooves management to find ways in which real information can flow as freely as is sensible and to encourage as much upward flow (two-way communications) as possible. Remember, too, that despite the formal organization chart there is an invisible and superimposed informal organization which will build its own channels for the flow of information, real and imagined.

Cutting across the departmental, divisional, or other structural separations of your organization are other ways of arranging people. These separations are, in fact, the informal organizational units. Every organization has its own unique properties, but some of the common "combining" factors for informal sub-units are identified and discussed in the following two paragraphs.

The old group versus the new. This division into sets might be related to something specific, like a take-over date when there was a merger or acquisition. Or it may simply be related to certain products or markets...before we expanded to a national company, after many years as a purely regional company, for instance (see the case study at the end of this book). Old versus new culture-bound groups will inevitably communicate across formal divisional lines and within the old-new configuration. There is a certain security in maintaining these ties that is also partly immature. Mature managers will open up strong channels which diminish the significance of the other dividing cultures and will reward and encourage people to break the informal ties to some degree.

Those with a certain ethnic commonality. Actually, any cultural dimension, including ethnicity, can build ties stronger than the formal ones in an immature organization. Other possible bases for informal and cultural bonds (and communications channels to develop) are: certain college experiences; military experience; regional origins, even within the same nation; male versus female. All such bonding is harmless so long as it is not subjectively defensive. That is so long as it is not fortified, or induced, by feelings of frustration or exclusion from being treated in immature ways. The brief suggestions contained herein and indeed all the maturity recommendations of this book, are suitable approaches for decreasing the likelihood that people will "retreat" into some informal enclave of comfort, for communications and a sense of belonging and power. But, and this is most important, the improvement process must be pervasive, wide-ranging, consistent and long lasting, to have the desired effects.

If there is one subject attempted in this book which has more significance than any other, then it is communications. Immaturity in communications is rampant, yet within the guidelines I suggest there are real possibilities for upgrading the whole organization. The next few chapters add a few dimensions with those very objectives in mind.

CHAPTER 6

Hiring, Evaluating, Appraising Performance

In the processes addressed in this Chapter lie the greatest threats to organizational effectiveness, for these are the arena's in which immaturity tends to dominate. Too many people are appraised as though they were not in a real relationship with others, especially not with "the boss." Similarly, a lot of dancing and posturing takes place in the hiring process, much of which gets in the way of real understanding and the vital objective of matching and of building a truly effective team relationship.

HIRING

The old-fashioned concept and practice, in some cultures, of Match-Making was inevitably based, more often than not, on very real and pragmatic issues such as size of dowry and the resultant building of synergies between families. Not entirely without just causes, the practice has long since faded from use in modern Western cultures. Instead individuals make their own "matches" based on more personal and more selfish needs. I would be the last person to suggest a return to social match-making, but I do urge that organizational hiring processes be seen from that point of view. There is the greatest chance of consistently successful outcomes when hiring is seen as synergistic match-making.

It is true that most job applicants are likely to have very selfish desires and goals for themselves, but the degree to which a candidate is willing to acknowledge the mutual dependencies gives many indications of real worth to the selection process. There are "givers" and "takers" in every organization; the degree to which you are able to build a team made up, primarily, of givers, is the real barometer for high potentials and a mature organization. Winston Churchill once said "We make a living by what we get... but we make a life by what we give." I am convinced that Churchill did not exclude giving of things other than those of monetary value. We all have a great deal to give to our workplace. Our energies, our creativity, our enthusiastic moral support, our long-term commitment. If an employee on any level is attuned to the question "What's in it for me?" then the battle to include that person in the maturity building process can be very challenging, in extreme cases a lost cause. So the first edict related to hiring is:

EDICT NO. 10:   MAKE THE FIRST CRITERION FOR HIRING THE WILLINGNESS OF THE APPLICANT TO GIVE OF THEMSELVES.

In any hiring situation, especially in positions for which there is a shortage of talent properly trained, there is a tendency for us to assume that the most important criterion is the fit of expertise and experience. We also, most of us, have this enormous ego that tells us that we have the ability to motivate and lead in such a way that even the "difficult" employee will respond favorably to our strong leadership. I do acknowledge that much individual growth can take place in the right environment but I insist that you will find it easier to develop expertise in people than it is to change attitudes. Hence the first edict on this subject, above.

On the other side of the hiring issue, of course, the candidate needs to see, very clearly, the attitude of the organization; in other words, the climate and culture of the place and the department. It is your responsibility to fully understand these things, especially in terms related to maturity, and to honestly convey the truth. If you are working towards goals in this respect, tell of your progress and your aspirations, also tell of the failures, thus far. Depending upon the level of maturity in the candidate, and the level of the position within your organization, solicit their understanding and opinion on how to make further progress. Do not be afraid to show your own vulnerability. In the interviews be "up-front" about what you expect from the person placed in the open position, especially in terms related to their role in building a mature team.

On these issues, there should be no room for guessing games, or games of any kind. The most direct and honest approaches are essential. These factors are more important to both parties than any other consideration!

In those aspects of matching applicant skills and training to the duties in the position, remember that ALL positions take on new dimensions to match the strengths and abilities of the incumbent. Only in the most Mechanistic and Bureaucratic organizations are there expectations that a JOB DESCRIPTION accurately describes and prioritizes the work, duties, responsibilities and outcomes for each particular worker. In more organic entities, outcomes of the collective are assured by appropriately filling the organizational positions with regard for everyone's ability to contribute. Good football coaches know the wisdom of selecting good athletes with great attitudes, then deciding how they fit together is a secondary consideration. I realize that even in football, there have to be some with specialized strengths and skills, and so it is in any workplace. But the fundamental wisdom still applies. This leads to the second edict:

EDICT No. 11:   DO NOT PLACE TOO MUCH EMPHASIS ON THE JOB DESCRIPTION.

In some organizations, individual job design is so focused that people are seen more like pieces of a jigsaw puzzle than flexible dynamic performers. Remember, if a job description is precise enough to define specific tasks and responsibilities, it is also precise enough to explicitly limit people, preventing their horizontal growth. It is also limited enough to prevent the dynamic interaction effects to produce real human synergies. The old saying, "That's not my job man..." comes from attitudes directly related to the rather silly notion that in order for an organizational unit to function effectively, all individuals must know exactly what they are supposed to do, and what they are supposed not to do. It may well be that a major military incursion depends on such bureaucratic and structured understandings, but most organizational entities would suffer shortfalls in performance and severe discouragement among workers, under these constraints. This is especially so where the environment is dynamic, because rapid change necessitates a changing role for virtually everyone. The degree to which you and your organization mature determines the degree to which the collective ensures that all tasks are taken care of and the extent to which the organization recognizes, pro actively, the looming challenges and opportunities.

In the approach that I recommend, there is potential danger, of course, that some aspects of the work would be left undone. The key to this, again, lies not in having individuals who are assigned such tasks individually, with the full complement covering all bases as discreet parts of the whole. Instead, the collective recognizes what must be done, and therefore each individual does too, and the collective assumes responsibility for the outcomes, for goal attainment and for even the most distasteful of tasks. A healthy and mature group will find its own way of dealing with unpleasant tasks under the following circumstances:

1) There is a clear understanding of the goals;

2) There is a shared approach to the setting of goals;

3) Rewards/Acknowledgement comes to the group as a whole;

4) Leader maturity is being demonstrated most of the time.

The only alternative to this collective interactivity is to have an omnipotent leader... as you must know, this is highly unlikely in a complex organization. On the last item, as was mentioned in an earlier chapter, the best of leaders are not perfect. Mistakes will be made, but so long as there is a dominant pattern and so long as there is appropriate acknowledgement of the mistakes they will not impair your leadership.

Using a common experience from everyday life, to illustrate my last point: consider what can happen in a large extended family gathering where there is a major meal served. There are many chores involved in preparing the meal and in serving it and clean-up afterwards. Mature and integrated families find a way to get all these chores handled with minimum fuss and rancor. Some individuals (less mature ones) do not make an equitable contribution, others carry larger than fair burdens, but this is a situation where there are no job descriptions and no (formal) bosses. For the most part, also, family members have not been chosen to round out the team. I hesitate to suggest that organizational units are like families - this is such an overdone notion - yet in some ways they really are.

The point is that selection of employees must be seen in a system-wide context. Matching up individual strengths with specific tasks to be performed is only satisfactory at the very lowest and task-intensive levels of your organization. This is perhaps one of several reasons that assembly-line work and similar manufacturing environments are so often discouraging. Even as individuals, people need to feel some freedom of choice and action, some sense that they can, some of the time, escape to slightly more creative and flexible pursuits. If they do not have this opportunity within their range of responsibilities they will take such excursions in their minds, daydreaming, etc. This means they will be considerably distracted, accident prone and frequently absent, physically as well as mentally.

The hiring process is one which calls for you to thoroughly prepare yourself. Even the most experienced interviewer is likely to fall into the trap of assuming that their experience will carry all interviews to successful conclusions. You must know exactly what the state of your organization is, what the realistic perceptions are in terms related to maturity and its progression (or otherwise) and how you are going to evaluate applicants given the position and status you now have, and the "state" of the organization. Take the risk of including in this development of total understanding several people in your organization (before defining the hiring procedures and criteria). Rotate this involvement so that it is not seen as "for the chosen few." Include also, some other people in the interview process; not just simply to get their "input," but so that they and the applicant get a sense that this really is an integrated organization and learn something about the progress and the needed further development.

"Realistic Job Descriptions" are referred to in all modern Human Resource text books, and there is some wisdom in the recommendation for their development and use. But at least of equal importance is that you, and most others in your unit, come to grasp the significance of potential synergies and other dynamics attached to a given position and any new person which will be filling it. These understandings must be a central part of the discussions before, during and after the interviews with candidates. Listen very carefully to what the included people say. Watch for opportunities for recognition that their contributions are valued, and deliver that recognition! Watch, also, the growth and maturation of the people you involve in these processes, and for their continuing interest in seeing that the final outcomes prove to be positive. These simple inclusions do much more than ensure the best possible hiring results, they also assure a gradually maturing organization.

I do not, here, intend to deliver a full range of suggestions for questions to ask candidates, how to check references, or the many other items on a typical check-list for effective hiring. These things are readily available in Human Resource Management textbooks, etc. This manual is intended to focus on aspects of management maturity and on guidelines not typically found in text books or taught in management classes. Suffice to say, here, that during all contact with candidates, mature managers AVOID DOING the following things:

1) Do not use the time with candidates to impress them with your own importance or ability;

2) Do not play mind games, asking questions the answers to which you yourself cannot directly use in your assessment;

3) Do not paint an untrue rosy picture of organizational bliss and success, or similarly of the assignment being filled;

4) Do not tell the candidate YOU are the one who will be making the hiring decision, unless it is true;

5) Do not prevent the candidate from telling their story;

6) Do not withhold information which would help the candidate try to match their strengths, appropriately, to the assignment;

7) Do not use up most of the time with "your" story;

8) Do not fail to tell the candidate how much time is available, who they will talk with, and other details and arrangements for their evaluation either <u>before</u> they arrive or as soon as they first arrive;

9) Do not fail to have a general plan for the interview itself and to outline that plan early in the meeting;

10) Do not be so rigidly attached to all plans that you cannot allow the applicant some sovereignty of their own, to influence the direction and conduct of the interview;

11) Do not fail to indicate to the applicant what will happen next; how soon a decision will be made, who will contact them, who they should contact for any of their own follow-up needs, etc.;

12) Do not hesitate to tell applicants what your first impressions are; comment on strengths or other characteristics which please you, and why, and comment, briefly, on any concerns you might have, giving them the opportunity to respond.

Interviewing is an art and a science. You can learn many skills associated with developing understanding of other people, of course. But the most important ingredient in effective assessment of others is in being open, taking risks, avoidance of "games," being fully pre-pared, being relaxed, being, in these and all other ways, MATURE.

One final point on the hiring process, try to get your own mental attitude on hiring, and that of your key people (at least) to a state which acknowledges that hiring is not something one does when there is a vacancy. Instead, get to an operational state of <u>readiness</u> to hire by doing the following four things constantly:

1) Have, in general terms, a specific inside person in mind as a potential candidate for <u>every</u> position in your unit;

2) On the above item, don't automatically assume that every move by someone should be a "promotion." Cross-training and horizontal "promotions" have tremendous value in a mature organization;

3) Be on the alert for recruiting opportunities at all times, <u>especially</u> when there is no current opening;

4) See that all your people are "tuned-in" to this same hiring philosophy. . . pro-actively thinking of the need for good people, all the time, not just when "needed."

EMPLOYEE EVALUATION

I must confess that I have a very simplistic notion about performance appraisal: If the organization is functioning as it should (maturely) then performance appraisal rituals, forms and procedures are not necessary. Let me hasten to add that I fully understand that every (large, complex) organization has inevitable bureaucratic requirements (see Chapter 4 again) and that files must be kept to provide information to people who may not have direct contact and familiarity with the performance of people (when considering transfers or in other exceptional circumstances). In other words, I know that certain realities dictate a somewhat procedurally oriented, consistent and formal performance evaluation program.

Notwithstanding the needs of the organization to protect itself, or to improve overall performance and to be fair and consistent in the treatment of people, the MOST important reason for performance appraisal is so that individuals <u>who work together</u> can:

1) Be recognized and fairly compensated or rewarded based on some very well understood criteria related to the specific functions of the unit involved;

2) Better perform, together, the collective assignments that take the organization or sub-unit toward identified goals. And, indeed, the improvement in identifying and clarification of these goals;

3) Provide each other with information which will, or can, improve some aspect of the operation or of the work being done, or possibly the levels of satisfaction, or which can reduce the levels of frustrations;

4) Give the workers affirmation of their own growth and development, as a base for their progress toward their own individual goals and aspirations.

Now, hopefully, readers may grasp the bases for my overstatement which opens this section. The MOST important outcomes of well developed performance appraisal systems are UNDERSTANDINGS which develop between people who must work together in some common causes. Anything which ritualizes (bureaucratizes) these understandings, or which places emphasis on the formalities (forms, files, due dates, etc.,) has high potential for diminishing the real value of open and continuing communications between highly interdependent people in work settings.

It would be very unlikely that two married people could develop a valuable "appraisal" system, each for the other, if it depended on the following common workplace appraisal elements:

1) A due date for the appraisal interview;

2) Forms to be completed as part of the appraisal;

3) Labels such as satisfactory, unsatisfactory, good, outstanding;

4) Discussions of compensation changes as a result of good performances.

Yet, as you all know, these are indeed some of the commonly seen aspects of performance appraisal, which, on their own can do much to diminish the real value of MATURE UNDERSTANDINGS among close workers. But there is an exacerbating factor which makes the situation even worse. I refer, of course to the likelihood that "the boss" doesn't even really know much of the detail of what each worker does. The reason for this, remember, is that in the typical vertical promotion path people by-pass many (perhaps most) functional areas. How the devil, then, could "the boss" come to know much of the day-to-day challenges faced by each worker, except in the case of very task (and product) oriented assignments.

I am not advocating that "bosses" therefore should spend major blocks of time becoming familiar with the specifics of each worker's daily routines. Cross-trained "bosses" certainly do have an advantage here, however. Instead, I urge the following:

1) Make sure that your appraisal system includes a major component of self-appraisal. That is, encourage self-set goal development and refinement with continuous opportunity for revision/upgrade;

2) Devote more time to developing group goals (group-set) and to group self-evaluation (Deming says that we should never evaluate individuals!);

3) Do not assume that all that needs to be communicated about performance can be done in a meeting once-a-year, every six months, every three months or even monthly;

4) Avoid adherence to rituals, especially avoid saying things like. . . "I suppose we must get your performance appraisal done soon...;"

5) Be open to the notion of MUTUAL appraisal, continuously.

On several of these points, let me expand, because there is enormous benefit to be gained in these critical approaches to maturity. The first one, involving self appraisal, is terribly critical. All of the literature on MBO's (Management by Objectives) clearly shows that MBO systems fail unless a major part of goal-setting is done by the subordinate. There is under such constraints, failure of the system. There is nothing quite so inspiring to a worker as the challenge of determining the specific what's and how's related to an assignment. With maturity, this can even be improved upon by linking the individual worker's "What's" to those of others in the unit. It is only the most immature individual who will tolerate being told what to do and how to do it. . . and we want much more than just "tolerance" from our people, we want commitment.

This is a good time for a short theoretical excursion, on the subject of employee commitment. Followership can exist on three theoretical levels:

COMPLIANCE

IDENTIFICATION

INTERNALIZATION

With mere compliance, the least mature of responses to leadership, there is nothing more than simple, uncommitted adherence to orders. Minimum standards will, or can, be met, but those operant under this level will not seek ways in which to excel. Nor will they find new and creative solutions or be proactive in identifying opportunities and threats.

Employee followers who can and do IDENTIFY with goals, instructions and standards will need less of the leaders time and energy in coaching, etc., but will not be fully proactive in their own search for improvements or in helping others to mature.

When followers actually INTERNALIZE the philosophy, standards, approaches and goals of the leader, there is the greatest likelihood that all the advantages of a mature organization will be realized. There is every expectation that such people will not only seek and find solutions to problems but will also identify problems before they are manifest. They will also be likely to assist other employees reach this desirable level of maturity. Remember, though, these are all possible reactions to your own maturity OR LACK OF IT! This is not only true for your methods of appraisal, but also of all your other leader behaviors.

EDICT No. 12:   MAKE GOALS FLEXIBLE AND, IN PART, SELF-SET.

The flexibility of self-set goals is so very important. The slow realization that a goal is just simply not reachable is the greatest demotivator I know, for such are straight-jackets to creativity and enthusiasm. Some goals can and must be changed to suit rapidly changing conditions. To lock-in to annual goals which no longer make sense is immature. It has always amazed me, in countless tests of this, that people who work in a mature and open environment will set <u>higher goals</u> than those I would have set for them! And, most importantly, because they themselves set those goals, they have a special interest in seeing that there is goal attainment!

This, of course, does not mean that all goals should be self-set, and the level of maturity and experience should dictate the aggressiveness of this program. But be assured that on every level in your organization, there is much to be gained from this aspect of participation by workers, especially if you can develop non-rancorous and unselfish group goal-setting and group self-appraisal.

I realize that forms often need to be "filled-out" to complete certain ritualized aspects of your organization's appraisal system, and, indeed, adjectives used to describe the worker performances. Make no mistake, I am not advocating just "plugging in" any old information to get these forms completed on time. Make certain, in fact, that information that is recorded on any form is factual and thoroughly representative of the understandings you have with all your people as individuals. What I am saying, however, is that the form is incidental to the process, not central to it; and so is the appraisal interview itself. I insist that if a worker needs to be "interviewed" to discover how they are doing, or to provide you with information on how <u>you</u> are doing, then you are not a manager at all! Just as in the silly notion of appraisal systems for married couples (above), there must be constant, on-going, open, honest and sincere communication ALL THE TIME about how the relationship is progressing. When that is the case, the forms and the rituals are relatively insignificant and non threatening. When the continuous dialog is not open, then forms, appraisal dates etc., become very threatening and unproductive.

On the subject of separating the discussion of compensation from discussions of appraisal, I realize I am suggesting something very difficult. Remember, though, that money is both an instrument and a symbol. As an instrument, people use it to obtain items which satisfy fundamental and complex needs. There is, within the realm of motivation literature, much which suggests that money is NOT a motivator. If you accept the notion that all motivation is intrinsic (see Chapter 2, again) and that externalities are merely rewards or punishments, you may understand that the SYMBOLIC nature of money is far more complex than its instrumentality. To a considerable degree, a salary increase (above and beyond cost-of-living increases) can symbolize recognition, appreciation, growth, progress...all of which are related to internal feelings capable of raising levels of motivation and commitment.

When my students ask (as many do) "is money a motivator?" I tell them to read the motivation literature and then tell me their answer. It is not an easy question to answer. There is no question that there are many variables affecting worker motivation and that compensation levels (comparative and absolute) are intricately woven into the formula. Equity, or rather inequity, is a major concern for most people, even the very mature. One does not have to be looking "over the shoulder" of a fellow worker all the time to, nevertheless, be making comparisons and trying to ascertain relative "value," in other words, making certain there is equity in compensation, among other things. Such concerns are capable of demotivation, surely.

For all these reasons, I offer. . .

EDICT NO. 13:   DISCUSS SALARY ADJUSTMENTS ON A
                 SEPARATE OCCASION!

(But make sure everyone knows, in advance, this will be the way that evaluations are handled.)

I advocate discussing specific salary adjustments separately from performance for a variety of reasons. If, as I recommend, you have open and continuous communications which leads to consistent and clear understandings about performance then the separation of compensation is NOT a problem. If, on the other hand, there is that dreadful uncertainty, by a worker, about "how they are doing", until the appraisal interview, then the money inevitably becomes the central issue in their mind. Also, if the "final act" in their performance appraisal interview is known to be the discussion of money, employees will be influenced by that agenda item throughout the discussions. This is not conducive to frank two-way evaluation.

Mature workers should be compensated fairly and equitably,

they should be told the details of your own difficulties in negotiating on their behalf (or for the total package of compensation changes). They should be told the range of adjustments across all the workers in your unit, and, in most cases, your own salary adjustment, in general terms. All these discussions should, I feel, be handled in an entirely separate meeting from the one in which you affirm understandings (mutual) about performances. Above all, you should be honest about what you think and feel about the level of compensation for each individual worker. It is amazing how workers come to respect and trust "bosses" who are open and honest in this way. By contrast, it is amazing how, over time, respect dissipates for "bosses" who attempt to con workers into believing all kinds of claims, especially those involving compensation, by bosses who are weak, less than honest and open... the IMMATURE!

Evaluation processes, and those surrounding recruitment and hiring, are the arena's of enormous immaturity. Make a decision, now, to advance your own maturity, and that of your organization, by adopting the suggestions and guidelines offered in this chapter.

REPRIMAND and CENSURE

Even in the best of organizations, and with the best possible approaches to hiring and promotion, etc., there are inevitable performance problems which must be dealt with in a mature fashion. Sometimes, a well handled reprimand will produce very positive turn-around and a new level of commitment (though if everyone were really mature this could not be the case).

As has been stated and implied throughout this book, the system wide effects of leader behaviors (especially) are often nearly invisible, potentially very dangerous and need to be prevented or fully understood. When someone is NOT performing well there is an expectation by others, who are, that you will deal appropriately with the errant party. For this reason, though the whole process must be conducted in private, the general spread of knowledge that the needed reprimand is being handled, and that you intend to follow through on all aspects, is a critical "informal" set of communications you want to happen. However, note my point about privacy and the following:

EDICT No. 14:   AVOID REPRIMANDS OR SIMILAR FORMS
OF CRITICISM IN PUBLIC.

No matter how bad the performance or what the circumstances of discovery of a problem, you must permit the errant worker the dignity of privacy. Not only is this important in saving a possibly good relationship with the worker in question, but all other workers "get" the message that you respect "Them!" This is a vital ingredient in the processes of leadership and communication and a huge determinant of your level of success in building and sustaining maturity.

EDICT No. 15:   NEVER REPRIMAND FOR THE FIRST
FAILURE (of a particular kind)!

Short of dishonesty (stealing, malfeasance, etc.) no-one should be reprimanded, or anything close to it, on first failure. All continuing efforts to build an effective work team, however, are dependent on you, or someone else on the team, pointing out the problems caused or potentially caused by the error. A most important part of the disclosure is also the coaching and questioning to ensure that the person committing the error is armed well enough (information or skills) to avoid repetition. To fail on this last item is to guarantee frustration, nervousness or timidity - all characteristics to be avoided in the mature organization.

Not only are there legal requirements to ensure fairness in handling errant employees, there are also maturity requirements which are very similar. Any attempts to correct errant behavior or performance must follow the guidelines listed in the following giant, collective, edict:

EDICT No. 16:   REPRIMANDS REQUIRE THAT YOU. . .

1) Be absolutely certain of all the facts;

2) Give the person(s) involved every opportunity to explain their position before delivering any edicts or demands;

3) Be certain that the person(s) involved know exactly why there is a problem, be specific about outcomes, etc.;

4) Give every opportunity for the person to identify specific needed help, instruction, tools, etc.;

5) Disclose exactly what you intend to do in follow-up (how monitoring will be handled, and by whom);

6) If the problem is serious enough, specify exactly what will happen in the case of repeat problems;

7) In the case requiring monitoring, if by someone other than yourself, bring that person into the picture early enough for them to make useful suggestions;

8) When appropriate, give time to the offender to make adjustments. Be sure that this time-frame is clearly understood;

9) Follow-up <u>personally</u>, whether there is evidence of need or not;

10) Document all understandings and be sure that all involved parties have copies of the documentation.

In addition to the foregoing general guidelines, there is one other kind of progression, that which involves your trappings of power and authority. In the earliest phases of a reprimand (except of the most serious kind) you must NOT use all your arsenal of power. Instead, begin in a very personal way, away from <u>your</u> desk and office and using only personal power bases. If there is need to reprimand a second time, or if the event is truly heinous the first time, then all guns must be used including all the architecture and formality of your office. In such circumstances, you are not a person, but an "officeholder!"

TERMINATIONS

Bringing to a close the unsuccessful process of reprimands by ending the relationship with an employee who has failed to measure up to requirements and expectations is one of the most difficult tasks of the manager. The reason for this difficulty is that, in essence, it is an affirmation of your own failure. You made a mistake in hiring, in promoting, or in developing someone you previously expected to do well. If you can get your own ego out of the way in this, however, it can be a growth opportunity for you and an affirmation of your leadership. The guidelines involved are exactly like those for reprimand, above, only they include the one final step. Learn from your mistakes, try to ensure that others around you learn, also, and that there is widespread appreciation for what has happened, why it has happened and what can be gained from the experience. Be sure that everyone even slightly involved helps provide insights on how to proceed without making similar mistakes.

The following chapter attempts to show how to extend the maturation process, once progress is made, to real organization-wide progress and growth.

CHAPTER SEVEN

Maturity, Democracy, Interdependence

What they have to do with Organizational effectiveness

The edicts, suggestions and ideas contained in the pages of this book are related concepts all of which are tied to the notions of maturity and the modern (late 1980's) management fad called "empowerment." They are also related to the much more solid management concept called "Systems Approaches." I have stayed away from using the term empowerment for a deliberate reason: it tends to inculcate some wrong assumptions about power. Before going any further, let's return to previous discussions about power (see pp 33-35). The key points to remember are that there are different sources of power, that each of these sources provides a kind of power that is not universally applicable and that all of them are dependent upon the person in the power position receiving power from another individual or group. This was referred to by Chester Barnard as "Acceptance," I make this a more active concept by labeling it "assignment." It is simply an acknowledgement that any potential influence any one person has over another, is assigned to that person by the one under influence. I realize that there are some circumstances, and indeed culturally induced attitudes, which minimize any individual's appreciable ability to actually allocate power to others. My students always, and quickly, argue that if one is in prison, for example, one has little choice but to respond to the power of the captors. My response sometimes is hard to grasp, and is not entirely without difficulty and counter-argument but let me try it on you.

There is a wonderful and true story of the indomitable human spirit, the Birdman of Alcatraz. Imprisoned for life, in Alcatraz, Robert Stroud found a way to ignore or overcome his apparent powerlessness in many dimensions, and concentrate his energy and resources in one particular way; the study of ornithology. Oh, it didn't start out that way, but his boredom in general and the appearance of a wounded bird on the window-sill of his cell, led, ultimately to a thirty-year concentration on birds, their anatomy, etc. It could just as easily have been any other intellectual pursuit, but the choice made by Bob Stroud was to concentrate on the study of something very specific. The point is that one is "in prison" in a total sense, only if one resigns oneself to the physical constraints and ignores the relatively limitless intellectual capabilities and choices of the human mind. There are countless other stories, one doesn't have to look very far for evidence that power is indeed a relative thing and that each of us chooses how much of our own power to give, or assign, to others.

Notwithstanding the foregoing assertions, the notion of employee empowerment through delegation is a valuable one, but there's a catch or two. The primary catch is that there must be a reasonable match-up between the level of power/autonomy delegated and the MATURITY, or readiness of each and every employee in every organization, and these factors are dynamic, they change with time and with the assumption of power. As I said in a prior chapter, every manager has a responsibility to create appropriate "Match-ups" of all kinds. When an organization has few, or as few as possible, mismatches, there will also be a low level of frustration. The potential frustrations are of two general types: the first is the sense of powerlessness which comes when employees are treated as though they were insufficiently mature; the second, and equally damaging, comes when people have been entrusted with decision making authority beyond their expertise, experience and confidence.

The second of these two organizational mis-matches is really quite rare, at least as spelled out here. A slightly different form of this problem, however, is not so rare. Management incompetence in some particular functional area, often for good and valid reasons, can lead to a form of abdication. As the theory books tell us repeatedly, delegation becomes abdication when the delegator withdraws from oversight and advisement roles for any reason. No matter how mature one's people, delegation of responsibility is not possible! It is only possible to delegate a form of authority. For this reason, we must always remain fully in touch with what is going on, what decisions are being made, what outcomes are developing AND the degree to which the delegatee is also delegating. The accountability feature of the delegation equation cannot be overemphasized, hence the next edict:

EDICT No 17:   DELEGATE, BUT INSIST ON FULL
                 ACCOUNTABILITY.

One of the great repeat problems of American organizations, and one which occurs less frequently in Japanese companies, is that promotions come fast and tend to be vertically oriented. An American worker, unlike the Japanese counterpart, would not consider it rewarding to accept a lateral "promotion." I cannot tell you how many times I have heard young managers talk of a "within-company" change of assignment, declaring, "it just isn't much of a step up!" The Japanese manager would be proud to be given opportunity to learn another functional area of the business and to repeat these lateral moves until thorough exposure to all major functional areas is realized. This means that when the vertical move does come, ALL the people now reporting to the fully cross-trained manager would have the advantage of an experienced counselor, instead of only the relatively narrowly trained American-model manager. Not only are the obvious missing experiences a problem for manager and subordinates, but, the new and inexperienced person will tend to hold on to the reigns, tightly, in their own area of expertise AND tend to abdicate, in other areas, rather than display vulnerability or weaknesses in the functional area not experienced. This leads me to two edicts which are truly at the heart of all good mature management:

EDICT No. 18:   DELEGATE IN A WAY WHICH MATCHES
                 DELEGATEE MATURITY.

EDICT No. 19:   NO MANAGER IS EXPECTED TO BE
                 OMNIPOTENT, TO HAVE ALL THE
                 ANSWERS.

Think about this last edict for a moment, especially in connection with the notion of synergies and of acknowledged inter-dependency. What a boring world it would be, for workers everywhere, if the "boss" had all the answers! It is truly a foolish notion, isn't it? Even in the Japanese model discussed previously, the fully cross-trained person is not in possession of all the answers. In the case of American organizations, the more narrowly trained manager is not God, even in his or her own area of expertise! But many of us assume that we must be omnipotent or at least so well prepared and informed that we can deliver answers to most problems and questions. If indeed we do have high levels of expertise, the managerial responsibility is to develop competence among others, not solve their problems for them. All good managers must teach others those essentials necessary for their role fulfillment. As a matter of fact, the kind of growth in maturity I recommend must be developed by encouraging all subordinates, especially those who are managers on some level themselves, to develop their own solutions to problems, or at least an array of alternate solutions. The subordinate who comes to you "with a problem" is telling you, unconsciously, that indeed YOU are the problem. Instead of this approach for help they should come to you with the description of conditions needing correction and a recommendation on how to fix the situation. In the case where you have a long established level of confidence, in them and their maturity, it should even be that the "fix" has already been applied and you are informed after the fact! This, of course, calls for a great deal of trust; it is difficult to say whether trust causes confidence, but clearly there is a relationship, and a vital one, between these concepts. You may want to read the section on mentoring again, after absorbing the current section.

In an organization where everyone feels that they can make significant decisions, or at least influence them, we have the best possible chance of having workers excited about their work, the work place and the work team. Such teams are lively, responsive to external threats and opportunities, flexible and highly successful. As I declared in the opening chapter, one does not have to pass all decisions to employees all of the time for this workplace euphoria to exist. But there does have to be a significant amount of such empowerment and a match-up between the self-perceptions of maturity, by workers, and the degree to which they see that maturity being respected and used. There also must be a real sense of growth in this dimension.

Remember, it is a mark of your own strength and maturity to be able to admit not knowing the answer to some questions, even in your own area of expertise. The degree to which you are truly dependent on others, in life and in the workplace, may not be clear in your own mind, it is not something most of us think about or try to crystallize. Similarly, the degree to which others are dependent on you may be relatively obscure. The real key to maturity, in one's personal life, and in one's career, is in discovering, understanding and acknowledging the real nature of inter-dependencies. As you will discover, in a later chapter (Chapter 10), I am also convinced that this is the key to world order and peace. This is not only critical for individuals but also for groups, organizations and nations. Until large proportions of the population come to realize these truths, the selfish needs and pressures of independencies will dominate individual and collective behaviors.

The reality that no-one is omnipotent, and the willingness of mature managers to acknowledge this, is what lies behind the old (and valid) management axiom "good managers surround themselves with strong people, weak managers appoint weak (immature) people." I do not suspect that weak managers consciously appoint weak subordinates, and I do not think they do this with confidence that they can bring about significant change in weaker people. Instead, I am convinced that they do not have a good sense of their own maturity, strengths and weaknesses, hence they cannot identify the strengths and weaknesses in others very well. When they interview mature, strong, people, the signals they receive and the internal responses they feel are confusing and disturbing, because of their own immaturity.

I do acknowledge that there are a few people who do hire the relatively immature or even incompetent people with a conviction that their own strengths, as a leader/trainer, can bring about sufficient growth and improvement in people. But this is really a weak and ego-based assumption. Your people can learn more from their peers and from the system itself in a mature operation, than from you, in all but the narrowest of senses. Your role in this is to create the environment and to serve as a catalyst in the process, not to be the one who brings about the growth and maturity itself.

Your organizational unit can be an island of exceptional maturity and the results will be positive and remarkable, even in a larger organizational setting which is less than mature or is very bureaucratic. You have the most potential with those people we labeled your subordinates, but it doesn't end there. In Chapter Nine, we examine some simple ways in which you can help your "supervisor," and others not directly working with you, to mature, so that the entire organization develops in this way; a way that is loaded with potential for organizational effectiveness.

As was discussed in Chapter Four, there are certain features of an organization which either enhance or detract from attempts to build maturity in an organizational unit or team. If your organizational unit is geographically removed (decentralized) from others or from the "main" location, you have several advantages (and a disadvantage or two). The degree to which you conform to the central culture, in total, is diminished under these circumstances. Obviously, if the central culture is one which is highly power centralized (bureaucratic) you are more free to be substantially less so than you would be if located in the same building as all other operating units. To accomplish this variance, of course, involves some risks. First of all, your "boss," if perceptive, can discover a different atmosphere and climate. Other organizational functionaries (especially internal auditors) can also visit and "take readings" on the subject aspects of your organization and report on them. So what to do about these threats? I suggest you be the one to tell your boss, in advance, what your plans are (for developing organizational maturity) and why, perhaps even how, you are going to accomplish your goals. Ask for support, or at least understanding, and be very open (have him/her read this book!).

But I hear it now, your cries that your boss "would have a fit," or other claims that this approach may not be realistic, so let me add some cautionary guidelines. Bureaucrats cannot tolerate surprises, so do not attempt to unload the full extent of your decentralization (cultural change) plans all at once! Remember when you were a kid, and you wanted to do something you just knew your parents would not approve? Maybe it was the first sleep-over, or later, an overnight trip with other teenagers, not chaperoned. Well, even as a kid, if you were savvy, you did not dare unload on the folks all at once. You told only part of the story: you wanted to inculcate the idea gradually, so the sudden realization that you were no longer "just a child" could penetrate slowly, didn't you? I realize that the main reason for being so careful (then) was abject fear, but now you are more mature and more politically savvy, yet the same cautions apply.

The resistance felt by your boss will be based less on parental protectionism and more on just plain bureaucratic resistance, but the effect is just the same. Seek input, first of all, on the general notions involved in your plan (delegation and its advantages and maturity notions as spelled out in this book, etc.). Be sure that you are acknowledging the experience and wisdom of your fearless leader (see chapter nine on immature politics, however), also acknowledge, gradually, that the settings of the two locations are different, that the smaller operation is much more conducive to a different culture. Oh, and don't forget to stress the performance advantages you expect to realize. Do all of this slowly, over several weeks, or months, when things are going rather well and certainly not until you have proven yourself under the head-office rules.

On this last point, it brings me to an edict, rather different in concept and application from most of the others in this book.

EDICT No 20:   NEVER ATTEMPT TO CHANGE THE
RULES OF THE GAME UNTIL YOU
HAVE PROVEN YOU CAN PLAY BY
THE OLD RULES.

It has been said, often, that management is manipulative. While I do not deny that most behavioral approaches to management have certain characteristics of manipulation attached, there is one important difference. When you are "manipulating" in your managerial roles, you are open and honest at all times. This is especially important when managing <u>down</u>, it is also critical (and much more difficult) when managing <u>up</u>! As you develop your plan to change to a decentralized culture, making it more open, you must be as open and forthright as you can be. You could use such language as . . .

Mary (the boss), I have a tentative plan to build a highly effective work unit in Phoenix (or wherever) and as I develop the concept, I want to tap your wisdom and experience frequently to ensure that any deviances from the corporate culture are not too significant for you to be able to accept and to ensure that I do nothing without your understanding. There are risks involved, but I think, at this stage, that the rewards, for you, for me and the company will be worth those risks.

The specific language here, obviously, depends on personality, relationship strength, your own track record and the degree to which Mary feels secure. It also depends very much on timing, and calls for face-to-face communications (see Chapter Six again). Only you can determine the exact approach, but since you have been promoted (or appointed) to the management position, you have already developed and shown some of the skills and instincts necessary for this kind of upward management, Refine these skills, because the only alternatives are ugly: confrontation or subjugation!

Another key variable in building an effective sub-unit is the avoidance of what I call "Islandism." Poet John Donne (see Chapter Two) was absolutely right, "No man is an island," and neither is any group of people. Inter-dependencies of all kinds abound. The siege mentality, or "we versus them thinking" has no place in a mature world or a mature workplace. All of the organizations with whom you interact (customers, suppliers, creditors, etc.) can be helpful in building productive and progressive synergies.

Even in the wacky world of manufacturing the last several years have seen enormous progress in this respect. A major manufacturer can be highly dependent on a myriad of small suppliers for all kinds of items (it is not unusual for an automobile, for instance, to be more than half made by someone other than the company whose name appears on the product. In this particular industry, and several others, those suppliers are scattered around the globe, and this trend is accelerating). Tough competitive positions in many industries have dictated a mature approach which, unfortunately, was slow in coming into practice. Major manufacturing firms are bringing suppliers into the picture much earlier, more completely and more openly. It is not uncommon now to have engineers, planners, and manufacturing specialists from a supplier actually stationed inside the manufacturing plants and offices of their customer, and vice-versa. This acknowledgement of inter-dependencies came a little sooner in Japan, they were coming from so far behind (I contend) that their motivation to change in this mature way was very high. Additionally, Japan is an island nation with ancient origins of siege and confrontation, their internal focused inter-dependencies produced this and several other competitive advantages.

As an aside, it will be very interesting to see how Japanese businesses develop over the next several decades. The culturally induced maturity of one sort (internal inter-dependencies and group cohesion) is not so useful over international boundaries, and the Japanese are not so open in this respect..... but back to our topic. The lesson here is that mature organizations, increasingly, must find ways in which all employees can come to recognize the necessity of acknowledging inter-dependencies and acting, always, in ways which fortify the collective gains. In America, a nation founded on, and still very dependent upon, individual initiative and self-sufficiency, this is no easy task for any manager, especially in a complex organization. I do not advocate minimizing the relevance of individual initiative, far from it. In fact I am convinced that individual entrepreneurs will always be likely to produce significant new advances and products. Unfortunately (I hope that this is not too strong a word) most new advances need the capabilities of larger, more complex manufacturing and marketing companies to maximize potentials in the shortest possible time-frame. As the rate of technological change accelerates, this becomes even more the case. A good new product innovation not brought to major markets in a hurry can wither in the face of the next generation of products.

The complex organization is NOT the realm of rugged individualists. Instead it is a place where highly integrated team efforts and synergies produce maximum effectiveness. This is the realm of the mature manager who can build highly effective teams of people all sufficiently mature themselves to operate in the ways espoused in this book. The mature manager is not threatened by dispersed power, by decentralization, or even by the feelings of "looseness" which sometimes accrue to these forms of organization. The mature manager, also, does not pull back previously released powers in a major recentralizing effort just because there is some cyclical or other temporary setback. I cannot tell you how many times I have witnessed this phenomenon. As soon as the economy tightens, or a new competitive threat emerges, the insecure manager imposes more controls, centralizes or in other ways strives to get his, or her, hands on all the reigns. In tough times we must do everything we can to control costs without controlling the behaviors, efforts, creativity and maturity of our people. To do otherwise reverses real organizational progress made in the "good times."

I realize that managers on the lowest levels are "corks in the waves" especially when major shifts or threats occur. But lower levels of managers eventually become senior and top-level managers; they thus have opportunity to NOT follow some of the negative tendencies described above. Lower level managers also have an advantage over their colleagues in the senior ranks. At the lower levels it is much easier to evaluate the work of others because the work done is more likely to have significant "task" components. At the higher levels, specific and quantifiable goals notwithstanding, the "process" is far more subjective, tougher to define and judge. Maturity, as defined here, is even more critical at the highest levels. Progress through the ranks is a wonderful opportunity to think about and apply the maturity concepts before you reach ranks where it is most critical.

On the other hand, if we are not careful, we can reward people at one level for immature behaviors by promoting them to higher levels wherein maturity is most desirable. In the chapter which preceded this one, the focus was on Hiring and Evaluating people for maturity, a most critical set of activities which, I claim, are subject to more immaturity than virtually all other managerial assignments.

The following two chapters provide insight and guidelines for organizational leaders in a variety of situations, Chapter Eight being focused on Leadership Roles and the Macro-Effects on the organization as an entity. In Chapter Nine I discuss some specific challenges outside the normal range, including some special caveats about organizations disturbingly referred to as "non-profit" operations. I contend that all organizations seek profits (gains) of one sort or another. But in organizations which have less clearly defined goals (including many entities) there are some special challenges to be dealt with.

CHAPTER 8

Leadership and Mature Organizations

In some ways, readers may find that some aspects of the materials and ideas presented in this chapter seem to contradict some of the previously presented suggestions, but bear with me. Those who read "In Search of Excellence" may remember that one of the characteristics of excellent organizations identified in Peters and Waterman's book was the somewhat confused notion of "Simultaneous Loose and Tight Properties". My interpretation of their intended meaning for this is that any organization must, on the one hand, be "tight" enough to ensure that central goals and mission are clearly defined and followed. However, the mature organization must also take the risk of being loose enough to permit flexibility of action by people on all levels. This juggling act, of course, calls for very careful leadership, very mature leadership.

MATURE PLANNING

Let's look, first of all at the planning process, for it is a leader's first responsibility to ensure that appropriate planning is done. For all genuine managers then, the planning process should occupy significant blocks of time. At the highest levels of management, planning is the dominant activity.

But what is a PLAN? In essence, a plan is a DECISION MADE IN ADVANCE! Or a series of inter-related decisions.

What do we need to know in order to make such a decision? And what are the fundamental ingredients in a plan?

First, we need to know what we are trying to accomplish. This is represented, in all organizations, on the highest plane by the MISSION (or statement of PURPOSE) and some organizations are very good at identifying their mission and articulating it, others less so. If you find yourself (now) wondering if your organizational mission is clear enough to serve all operating managers and their subunits, take a moment to explore it, using the following criteria.

1) A mission must be enduring, a relatively unchanging philosophy, one which is not forced into changes by relatively spurious changes in your domain. If a new product introduction or changed stance by a competitor (for example) seems to force a change in your mission, then your mission statement is written on too low a level.

2) A good mission does not identify goals or set desired performance targets, for these are transient, subject to influence. Instead, the needs of a segment of society and how they can be filled are addressed. The particular strengths of the organization are spelled out, especially those strengths which define the role(s) to be played.

3) The roles to be played by the organization in pursuing its mission must be clear enough that operating managers can answer, for virtually every major decision, "does this (product, activity, policy, procedure, etc.) fit with our mission?"

4) A well articulated mission makes goal identification rather obvious. If you have difficulty identifying meaningful long-term goals, take a close look at your mission statement.

5) Despite the admonishment (in Number 2, above) about goals, per se, a good mission is, nevertheless, rather concrete. It does not use lofty or vague terminology and ideals. Instead, it talks of specific markets or ranges of products and their "fit," it identifies real opportunities and how the organization (in general) will take advantage of those opportunities. It includes, also, acknowledgement of all the <u>stakeholders</u>.

In item 5, above, there is an important reference to "stakeholders." In essence, stakeholders are those people who, on any level, have a "stake" in what the organization does, and how it does it. It should be obvious to everyone that this is a very large group of people for any sizable organization. Stakeholders can be divided into those with direct involvement and those less directly connected but nevertheless connected.

<u>Directly Connected Stakeholders</u>

Shareholders   Customers
Investors/Backers   Suppliers
Directors   (Including Creditors)
Employees

<u>Indirectly Connected Stakeholders</u>

Community Neighbors   Local Unions
Society at Large   (The local workers
                                are directly connected)

The mission, and certainly the policies which are developed under its broad umbrella, must acknowledge all of the above stakeholders, though not necessarily in order of importance as presented here. Any mission which leaves out any one, or more, groups of stakeholders represents an invitation for managers on all levels to be parochial and short-sighted. Peter Drucker reminds us that it is easy to focus on "doing things right" (efficiency measures); it is much more difficult, and I claim, more imperative in an inter-dependent and maturing world, to "do the right things." Examining the whole set of stakeholders in the planning process, is much more likely to bring to consciousness the full range of organizational inter-dependencies. If the mission and overall plans of the organization are inclusive in this way, then managers at all levels will seek the minor goals and lead people in the "right" directions more often than not. Without this Outside-In focus, managers at the lowest levels will have no alternative but to focus on efficiency measures and their own "island-like" activities.

The Management Planning Paradox
(Also called the Leadership Dilemma)

It is easy to plan (make decisions in advance) in a stable environment, but planning difficulty increases with the rate of change and turbulence in the environment. It is, however, in the most turbulent environment that careful planning is most needed.

There is, in addition to the paradox inherent in the foregoing statement, an exacerbating factor which all managers must come to understand. In turbulent (threatening) environments, organizations tend to become more CLOSED, in self-defense; exactly the wrong adaptive strategy or tactic. By closed, I mean the various dimensions of immaturity as dealt with here, but also the rather more extensive meaning, as in "closed" systems.

SYSTEMS THEORY

It is now time to take an excursion into the theory of systems, for all interactivity is highly related to the system effects. All modern managers must respect the system; this is really the meaning of inter-dependency, maturity.

The simple definition of a system as: a set of interrelated parts or components, does it little justice. Any device which has more than one component, any organization which has more than one person, any process which involves more than one act or actor, is a system. General Systems theory comes from the insights of a biologist and a philosopher. The biologist was Ludwig Von Bertalanffy and the philosopher was Georg Hegel*, both of whom argued that although we tend to want to study things in an exclusive way (biology, physics, chemistry, for example as separate studies), they really are not <u>independent</u> subjects. All, Von Bertalanffy argued, can be included in a <u>systemic</u> study which cuts across artificial barriers and which lose something of value in their separate treatment.

On the subject of organizations as systems, we can examine the work of Katz and Kahn, who defined organizations as <u>open</u> systems, so lets first examine, briefly, what is meant by "closed" systems. A closed system is one which does not have interaction, of any sort, with any other system. It should therefore be obvious to all of us that there is really no such thing! Even a spaceship circling the globe, even with telemetry not functioning, has some, though limited interdependencies or interactions. In more earthbound settings attempts to "close" a mechanical system (such as the cooling system of your automobile, for example) are not completely successful. From time to time we must open up the "closed" system, to add water, or antifreeze. And in any event there is slight intrusion of impurities, and the system must give off heat to its environment. . . the system is not really closed at all.

Human systems, especially those we call organizations, we are even less able to close. Secret societies are as closed as any organization can be, yet even these have inevitable leaks in their boundaries. In fact, utilitarian organizations <u>must</u> seek ways of allowing effective interface beyond their boundaries. The degree to which a business organization or a "service" organization of any kind successfully interfaces with clients, suppliers and other stakeholders, with resultant mutual enrichment or needs satisfaction, is in fact the only meaningful measure of the organization's effectiveness.

On the theory of this much has been written. Perhaps the most comprehensive treatment of this subject, however, is that by Katz and Kahn, who concluded that all systems have specific attributes, eight of them in fact; these attributes or characteristics are tabulated and discussed on the following page.

----

* Hegel's contribution was in asserting that "The Whole is
   Greater than the Sum of its Parts."

1) Goal seeking;

2) Holism, or boundary definition, limitation;

3) Hierarchy, or sub-system priorities;

4) Inputs and outputs;

5) Transformation, or throughput;

6) Energy (use and generation);

7) Entropy, or losses, degeneration;

8) Equifinality, or variety and choice of operation.

The open nature of the organization, open that is to a huge variety of externalities, each with different levels of urgency and priority, makes for the great difficulty all leaders and managers face. We must recognize that the interfaces between organizations and their environment and also between sub-units within the organization provide an enormous array of challenges. These challenges call for a level of pro-activity which in and of itself is dependent on the very nature of the interface relationships. Leaders who do not acknowledge that those people closest to the customers, for example, are best able to communicate with those customers, are missing the great significance of the systemic interface problem. And the internal (sub-unit) interfaces are no less a challenge than this.

As we examine the above list of attributes of a system, we can develop an appreciation for the complexity of managing in an organization, on any level. We must be aware of the system wide effects, of both the decisions we make and the changes imposed by externalities and by effects not consciously induced. All decisions have high potential for unintended consequences. The intended consequences of the decision are difficult enough to calculate and provide for, let alone the unforeseen. It is for this reason that leadership of the autocratic type is less likely to inculcate high levels of confidence and commitment in workers. Even more importantly, the degree to which those frustrated in this way even care about the efficacy of the interface communication is very low. Under these circumstances, any information obtained by these people in their attempts to scan and read the environment is going to be incomplete or unreliable. Let's now return to the decision making model which started this chapter.

GOALS

After establishing and coming to broad understanding of our mission, we must next identify meaningful goals. As stated above, goals become clear and meaningful only when the mission itself is very clear. However, establishment of goals without the involvement of the people who are responsible for goal attainment is not likely to be of much value. This would be akin to having football team coaches determining a game plan for next Sunday without (at least) the senior players, captains and quarterbacks being involved. And a football team is (at least during a game) an organization type in which everyone understands the goals! Imposing goals and strategies on workers without their playing a part in the development of the same, is a sure-fire way to turn off mature workers or retard the maturation process. It will not even excite the very immature. The only saving grace with the extremely immature workers is that they have an expectation that you (the boss) will operate this way, and their expectation is confirmed; they will do what they are told to do and little else.

Incidentally, the once highly popular management tool "Management by Objectives"(MBO) failed in so many situations because though there is certainly merit in having people know exactly what their goals are, and on the basis of what criteria their performances are to be evaluated, these are not sufficient. Without some autonomy in setting goals and some team involvement in this and the evaluation process, there is not maximal commitment to the "well understood" goals. I have often contended that MBO will work very well in only one set of circumstances. . . when all, on all levels, feel that their responsibility and authority match their own perceived level of skills, training and preparation. For this match-up to be seen, there must be appropriate challenges and opportunities and a real sense of involvement by the vast majority in the goal setting and evaluation processes. Under such circumstances ANY contrivance will work, so why not MBO?   Incidentally, modern devotees of MBO now promote team goal setting. . . this is really nothing more than the simplest level of maturity, as defined here.

A far better style of leadership involves input from all who will play a role, including not only the what, but also the how. Extensive research has shown that workers encouraged in this way, to decide and define goals and methods, remain committed to the objectives in a personal way. Though there is little evidence that satisfied workers are more productive, there is plenty of other evidence confirming:

1) Committed Workers are More Productive;

2) Committed Workers have Fewer Accidents;

3) Committed Workers have Less Absenteeism.

Also, there is some convincing evidence that Satisfaction may be an outcome of feeling productive, rather than the other way around. Your job as a leader is to provide every opportunity for all your people to be and feel productive. This, in turn will lead to high levels of commitment and the results you desire.

LEADERSHIP

Some people have argued that management and leadership are really different, have different objectives, use different approaches. It is not difficult to find this distinction being made in management textbooks and leadership literature. While I acknowledge that there are leaders who are not in managerial roles, I also contend that good MATURE management is what leadership is fundamentally all about. In other words one cannot be an effective manager without being a fine leader. I like very much what Peter Drucker had to say on this subject. . . after discussing the "nuts and bolts" and specific talents of effective leaders, he said:

The final requirement of effective leadership is to earn trust. Otherwise there won't be any followers; and the only definition of a leader is someone who has followers. To trust a leader it is not necessary to like him. . . Effective leadership - and again, this is old-fashioned wisdom - is not based on being clever; it is based primarily on being consistent.

Drucker apparently had been in conversation on this subject with a bank vice-president, who responded: "But that's no different from what we know about the requirements for being an effective manager."

Drucker's reply: "Precisely!"

To which I would add: this is the requirement of the MATURE MANAGER.

Now we know that we must have a mission, and we must set goals and establish methods and parameters (policy) which have been partly influenced by workers on every level, and to a level which matches their perceptions of their own strengths. But someone must make the difficult choices. . . and this calls for leadership. A leader, then, in this mature model, is not someone who makes all decisions and imposes them for immature workers to follow. Instead, the leader seeks information and advice from everyone and weighs it according to the relative maturity of the contributor. The leader also makes the tough choices between seemingly contradictory or conflicting endeavors, and in other ways prioritizes. This is called, in management texts, "Contingency Management". The contingency, of course, is, in part, the level of maturity of the followers. Hersey and Blanchard have an interesting way of applying this notion of contingency to maturity. They suggest that maturity may be defined as a combination of ability and attitude (willingness to accept responsibility).

While I fully agree with these authors that the level of delegation should match the level of maturity, I contend that their model of maturity may be flawed. A really able and willing worker may also be an independently oriented one. If that is the case, and I have personally worked with many such, the influences from that source will have selfish interests inherent. For this reason I would suggest including the criterion of inter-dependence acknowledgement. Then

the general guidelines for various stages of participation or delegation, as suggested by Hersey and Blanchard, are very meaningful.

CONFLICT

If you refer back to Chapter 4, you will find discussion of factors which enhance or detract from attempts to build maturity.   In
addition, there are the more personal and social factors of Perception,
Personal Power, Culture (Group Dynamics) and of course, Politics.
As stated in Chapter 4, culture gives any group its distinctive identity.
Cultural dimensions include all behavioral norms for a group including special language, views of everything, belief systems and values.
The greater the number of clearly identifiable sub-groups in an organization (or nation) the larger the number of frontiers.   Cultural rifts
between, say, the engineers and the sales force, or across any of the
many cultural barriers of an organization, are inevitable.   The ways in
which mature managers deal with the challenges involved are dealt
with in Chapter 4, but there are a few additional cautions here.
The greater the number of diverse groups, the greater the potential for conflict.   Ensuring clarity of purpose and goals is a strong
leadership requirement.   In some organizational settings there are high
levels of structural or operational inter-dependency; in others, particularly service and the so-called non-profit operations, inter-dependencies are at low levels or not in evidence.   This "loose coupling" reality for some leaders creates an enormous challenge.   In any setting,
however, mature leaders must lower the barriers between sub-units
(cultural clashes real or latent) by ensuring that all participants have
opportunity to, and rewards for, focusing on super ordinate (common)
goals.
This, then, brings into sharp focus the need for the mission to be
clearly articulated and the goals to be thoroughly understood at all
levels.   Without this one really effective tool for the resolution of
conflicts is removed.   I refer, of course, to the attempts to focus on
super-ordinate goals and away from individual or sub-unit goal differences.   As a result of this option being excluded, there is inevitable
focus on parochial concerns and objectives.   This, in turn, means that
any attempt to provide within group incentives will automatically

create difficulties. Some people see such "within group" incentive systems as useful in building competition. This is a noble idea but unfortunately the difference between competition and conflict is slight indeed, as may be understood from the following definitions.

Conflict:
> A situation in which people perceive that others are blocking their goal attainment.

Competition:
> The incentive of comparative performance in which one competitor does not block goal attainment of the other.

We can infer from this that golf is much more like Competition, players competing with each other could both very well achieve their personal best score and (short of some very uncouth and unacceptable behaviors) each not prevent the other from doing exactly that. Boxing, on the other hand, is definitely conflict, each combatant trying to literally hurt the other and in fact knock them out of competition.

Mature leaders may look for ways in which the positive effects of competition can be used but avoid anything involving conflict. The problems associated with this are that Politics, Perceptions, Immaturity and the structural conflict latencies abound. Consider the following example.

In an organization where the product sold is modified, or in other ways readied, for delivery to a customer, there have to be decisions made on priority if all products sold cannot be readied at the same time. Service department time devoted to completion of one task may preclude completion of another. If those who benefit from this are in "competition", but are also immature, they can respond to this challenge in one or more of the following ways:

1) Perceive incorrectly...that there is favoritism or something equally discouraging;

2) Exaggerate the importance of their own customer;

3) Play Politics in very immature ways;
    (see chapter nine)

4) Turn off.

   In either case, the interplay of these responses between the competing parties, the supervisor in the service department and the supervisor of sales, is likely to turn competition into manifest conflict. The point is that when this occurs, it is evident that the organization has not developed maturity. If you are the general manager in this scenario, you have not used leadership in decision making prior to the occurrence. You have, in fact, in addition to the general failure related to overall goal understanding, been responsible for inducing the conflict itself, structurally!
   Conflict that is actually manifest (behaviorally) must have gone through some prior stages. It can make itself manifest in a short period of time, or over very long periods. The form it takes is also very varied, but it always passes through development stages during which mature intervention might have been possible. Latent conflict is that which has potential for manifestation because of the structure (as in the example, above), the circumstances or the persons involved. Structurally induced, or circumstantially induced latent conflicts abound in complex organizations, indeed they are perhaps inevitable. Decisions made without system wide consideration are the chief problem (or in other words, failure to respect inter-dependencies fully). Those situations which involve personality (for individuals) or culture (for groups) are similarly difficult to identify, but management maturity calls for active attempts to prevent their existence or their manifestation. One would not place a lion in a cage with a lamb...at least not without ensuring that the lion is very well fed! (or unless destruction of the lamb is our objective!)
   Actually, personality differences and serious cultural clashes are only latent conflicts among the immature. But as I have repeatedly shown - maturity can be a relative thing, AND, circumstances can change anyone's perception, even one's values, temporarily. Your job as a mature leader, among the many things discussed so far, is to ascertain that inter-dependencies and common interests are consciously embraced by all. But especially you must "manage" this level of understanding among those you have placed, circumstances have

placed, or personality and/or cultural differences have placed in a position of conflict latency. Complete harmony is not necessary in any setting, but productivity based on real accommodation is! Effective leaders recognize potential conflicts and prevent their manifestation in firm, mature, equitable, consistent acts, decisions and reward systems.

Your organizational unit can be highly effective and productive only if all sub-units and all individual members are primarily interested in the entire organizational objectives. The level if maturity of everyone and the respect for the real but sometimes obscure interdependencies are the keys to this kind of effectiveness. Your role in elevating everyone to this state of maturity should by now be abundantly clear.

I hesitate to refer to any management challenge as "routine," though there are some kinds of situations which do occur with considerable regularity. So far I have been dealing with just such frequently-occurring challenges. There are, however, a few situations which are definitely not routine, by any definition of the term; the next chapter attempts to guide readers on a few of these. Though the fundamentals are the same as previously discussed, there are special circumstances which dictate a different consciousness, in some cases different behaviors.

CHAPTER 9

Special Problems and Challenges

MATURITY AND POLITICS

It has often puzzled me that so few words have been written on the subject of politics in organizations; so few attempts have been made to connect political theory with the complex collective called the organization. Early in the sixteenth century Niccolo Machiavelli wrote The Prince and there have been a couple of attempts to show how the Machiavellian notions of power in State leadership (Kingship) can be applied to the organizational setting. In addition, of course, the general tenets of democracy have been similarly connected to management/leadership choice and style. But when one considers that politics is, at least in part, about power and its use in common cause, it must then be recognized that political action and thought are essential and central components of all collective human endeavor. Machiavelli had a rather cynical view of human nature (some would call it a realistic view) which came, no doubt, from his observation of the various forms of corruption he observed in government and (especially) the Papacy of the time. In a sense, this is based on an "animalistic" assumption about human nature. Since the time of Socrates, and maybe before that, thinkers have suggested three alternative views of humanity. Animalism is one view, the other two "views" of human nature are, of course: Rational Man and Humanistic Man. Jean Jacques Rousseau (the late eighteenth century philoso-

pher) envisioned a level of compassion in man which sets us aside
from the other animals. Whereas the animalistic assumption of man
would explain human behavior as essentially self-serving, the human-
ist, compassionate school believes there is basic good in everyone;
that "good" makes itself manifest in love, compassion, caring, altru-
ism and philanthropy. On this kind of continuum it is difficult to
place the "rational man" notion, but presumably it can "fit" with
either of the other "schools." Later, of course, (in the late nineteenth
century) Sigmund Freud declared that all men and women are driven
by various mixes of three elemental characteristics. He labeled these
characteristics the Id (essentially animalistic), the Ego and the Superego (essentially rational). Whether any of these (or similar attempts to
describe human tendencies) have validity is not the question here.
Instead, at least for the purposes of prescribing appropriate leader
behavior, I need to emphasize that the one important ingredient in
building followership is TRUST. Trust, however, is a function of
circumstances and of maturity in follower and leader. Maturity of the
sort dealt with in this book, like all other dimensions of maturity,
takes time to develop, is not without periods of regression and takes
place in individuals, if at all, at different rates and to different levels.
This means that you will never have all your followers at the same
level of maturity at the same time. This, as anyone who has been a
parent of children of different chronological maturity knows all too
well, presents a few very special challenges.

Immature Politics

Immature Politics in organizations is the attempt to influence on
the basis of fundamental needs, the ones in Maslow's hierarchy identified as "deficiency" needs. It makes itself manifest in all those obnox-
ious behaviors we refer to as "sucking up." There is no doubt that
such behaviors are indeed influential, but with what kind of leader? If
anyone is influenced significantly in the workplace by insincere flat-
tery, for example, then that person is relatively immature. To the
degree that such people encourage or reinforce this kind of immaturity
in others and show it in their own responses, they are guilty of failing
to build maturity in their own organizations. Now the difficult part of
this prescription is in the reality that all of us can be immature some

of the time. This means that when we feel insecure, threatened or confronted with significant challenge, we are susceptible to the immature political maneuverings of others. Well this is the great opportunity for us to ascend the scale of maturity and force our rational (our superego) being to dominate our behaviors. Remember, any behavior will not persist if it is not rewarded in some way. You, as leader, have the responsibility to reject the immature behaviors of others. You also have the responsibility to internally reject your own immature responses and to help your followers mature. You can be sure that those around you will not grow unless you reject their immature political moves and also counsel them on what you observe in them, what you are doing (the process) and what they are expected to do in response. In this way you have the best chance of building their confidence and trust in you and in themselves. Note that it is not enough to merely reject or rebuff their immaturity, for this would discourage and frustrate...you must also educate! These behaviors are very difficult to accomplish, but the first step is in awareness, the second is in desire. If you really want your team to be productive, progressive, flexible, creative (in facing external threat and opportunity) you must first get them ready by building their maturity and their trust.

Mature Politics

Mature Politics then, by contrast, is the recognition of interdependencies and finding ways of building coalitions of support. In any organization, your ability to persuade your boss and others to follow your recommendations is NOT just a function of the quality of your ideas. A major part of the ability to influence is in building support across a broad base of other people. Collective power in most organizations is difficult to resist, even by the most potent of individuals. You must find ways, mature ways, of persuading others to support your causes. In the process, of course, most of them will expect your support on their causes. In Chapter Five this was discussed in another context, here it is an acknowledgement of the role of politics in achievement by anyone. Complex organizations are not the arena in which rugged individualists can ride roughshod over everyone else, or use their own personal or positional power bases to the exclusion of everyone else's. Progress made using such individual and independent methods MAY succeed for a while, but begets immaturity across and throughout the organization and is thus likely to bring about a general failure of the organization in dealing with the complexity of challenges in the modern environment.

This then, is a place for two new Edicts:

EDICT No. 21:   ACKNOWLEDGE YOUR POLITICAL INTER-DEPENDENCIES.

(In other words, do not indulge in the immaturity of independence)

EDICT No. 22:   DO NOT REWARD OR TOLERATE IMMATURE POLITICS IN OTHERS.

(Instead, openly coach people in how to grow out of such behaviors)

The Extremely Immature

Extreme forms of immaturity are relatively easy to recognize, once you yourself are tuned to this whole concept. The obvious "sucking up," as discussed in the previous section; blatant lack of commitment/enthusiasm; petulance and "poor-me" behaviors; blaming others, or failure to accept blame; absenteeism; these are all evidence of immaturity in followers. Do not forget, though, that your own behavior can be a major factor in the persistence of these. All behavior in a social context is both a stimulus and a response...as previously discussed. Your first responsibilities lie in excluding immaturity from the majority of your own behaviors and in NOT rewarding such behaviors in others (and tolerance is a form of reward in the absence of real discouragement). But there are also some direct interventions you can employ which will help most people break their own mold. Remember that people who are chronically persistent in negative behaviors may not be redeemable. Or to put it another way, if, after reasonable attempts to develop behavioral change, you see no real growth, then replacement may be the healthiest option. I do not believe that all people can be redeemed. Your failure to "deal with" errant or sub-par performances and behaviors in any of your followers is a very serious impediment to developing trust among the others in your group. Even for the very mature this failure can be very discouraging.

The interventions I suggest, in bringing about change, all call for a level of trust and confidence which comes from your own self-disclosure, willingness to acknowledge that you may not have all the answers and a general organizational climate of discovery together. Then, any intervention which is based on open communications (dialogue, rather than one-way exhortations) will be seen as an opportunity to grow, rather than a criticism or a threat. Readers should refer back to the section on evaluation of performance (Chapter Six).

There is one important caveat which must be added here. The world is made up of all kinds of people. Not everyone will become a Gung-Ho follower who will want to take on more responsibility, or fall in love with their work. Remember though, it is not necessary to have everyone so committed to their work that the entire team is made up of world-beaters. In fact, this is an unrealistic assumption about workers and could produce its own problems. Some people can give very fair value in the workplace, not be striving for individual growth/challenge and still be a very worthwhile team player. The only thing to insist upon, in valuing such people, is that they are not a negative force! This is what I call the "rotten apple" caution. One rotten apple in a barrel can indeed spread the rot. Those who are of passive value in performing their assigned tasks to acceptable levels must not, therefore, be a negative force. As the old saying goes..."either lead, follow, or get the heck out of the way of those doing both!" There are a couple of edicts related to this notion:

EDICT No. 23:   DO NOT LET PASSIVE FOLLOWERS EXIST IN LARGE NUMBERS.

EDICT No. 24:   DO NOT LET A PASSIVE FOLLOWER OCCUPY ANY KEY ROLE.
(One which has complex internal interfaces or leadership)

This last edict probably means that you cannot have a "passive follower" in a <u>line</u> position. But there may be assignments we would refer to as <u>Staff</u>, in which the losses or risks are minimal. Also, be mature enough to discuss with those you have identified as "passive followers," quite openly, their status, your position on this and acceptability of the situation, also stating in very clear terms that any change in their situation would be welcome, not necessarily demanded. This is all part of the maturity of you and/or designate. Develop this same openness with all your people, who knows, some who would otherwise remain "passive" may turn into some of the most committed. If indeed this does happen, celebrate openly...others may be induced to follow, but be very fair, even-handed in your treatment of such progress. It is all too easy to see, and praise, <u>progress</u> in some and ignore very steady excellence in others. Don't make this (immature) mistake!

MANAGING YOUR IMMATURE BOSS

Upward Management is a term which has crept into management literature in recent decades, it is an interesting topic. In days when managers were seen as those who tell people what to do and how to do it, there was no room for such a concept. As the world of work matures (oh so terribly slowly) this useful topic becomes ever more meaningful. Again, the key factor in being able to accomplish much in an "upward" direction, is TRUST. Trust, of course is borne of <u>confidence</u>, in this case there are four dimensions of confidence. First, you must have been able to persuade your boss that you are worthy of his/her confidence and trust. Second, you must feel confidence in your own abilities and maturity to provide upward influence of significant value. Third, you must have confidence that in taking the risks of upward influence, you do not place yourself in jeopardy. Finally, and this is the tough one for you, the "boss" must feel enough confidence in his/her own security that there is not a defensive response to your influence or input. Readers may want to refer again to Chapters Five and Six, particularly the recommendation that all appraisal systems should include opportunity for much mature and open <u>mutual</u> appraisal.

On the last point the formal appraisal time (as suggested else-where) is not the only time for discussion of performance...in fact it may not be the best time in a mature organization. All work-related discussion is a form of appraisal! All co-workers in the mature set-ting must accept the responsibility (and the risk) of gently broaching the subjects of how "we," collectively are doing....how our work, efforts, attitudes, behaviors affect each other. In the truly maturing unit this openness becomes routinized, is not threatening. The prob-lem is that the immature boss, or the one whose immaturity lags behind that of the followers, can (or, more precisely, the behaviors of whom can) throw a real curve at the team of followers. The unpre-dictability of responses, the insecurities exhibited and the lack of trust will tend to bring about immature responses in those among the followers who are most vulnerable. Because individuals mature at different rates, have different levels of insecurity, some can backslide under conditions not quite mature. The ways in which you must counter these regressions are very demanding upon you, but impera-tive for restoration of the maturity progression. They are as follows:

1) Concentrate your efforts on fortifying the mature behaviors
   in others, including your followers and your peers.
   Go out of your way to counterbalance the direct negative
   influences of the immature boss.

2) Identify and recruit members of the team to work with you
   in the efforts mentioned in item No. 1, above. Tell them
   exactly what you are "up to," and why.

3) Encourage peers who are also in leadership roles to do
   exactly what you are doing (all of this set of items).
   Again, tell them exactly what you are up to, and why.

4) Provide the boss with direct feedback on the effects being
   felt in individuals in your unit, being sure, in the process,
   that you describe (initially) immaturity of the responses,
   not the immaturity of the stimulus.

On the last item, I acknowledge the manipulative nature of this. The point is that the immature boss is not ready to face the fact that he is the problem. If he were, then maturity for him has progressed to the point where more complete disclosure (on your part) can be risked. Instead, in the early phases of this extremely difficult challenge, your only real hope exists in showing the boss that there are different levels of maturity (you must discuss what this means, in general terms, of course) by individual, and openly stating that you are attempting to counter the immature reactions among the relatively immature. Over time, he comes to realize that there is no threat. When you sense this has developed, ask for his/her help in this program, not, at first, by requesting attention to his/her problematic behavior, but only on the other side of the equation. Slowly, if you are supportive and do not play the "immature political game," the boss's confidence in you will build. There is a related edict, and this is the last one in this book:

EDICT No. 25:   YOU ARE AS GOOD AS YOUR CURRENT
                   BOSS SAYS YOU ARE.

An important follow-on to the above edict is the reality that the only way in which you can guarantee your boss will see you in a positive light is if your efforts make him/her look very good. In other words, in the very broadest sense, your job is to make your unit (and thus even your very immature boss) appear as successful as you possibly can. Sometimes this can be very galling, I know, but think of the alternatives: either you must decide to go to "war" with the boss or you must walk away. In the first of these choices, let's suppose that you have the ammunition to win. This is highly unlikely because if your boss has been getting away with serious immaturity, in an otherwise relatively mature management structure, what does this say about the next highest level manager? Well, either there is a very immature boss at that level, or one without the ability to judge, or one unwilling to act, either in replacement or improvement of your boss. If, then, you are successful in deposing your boss, or in discrediting him/her, do you think that an insecure higher-level manager is going to risk having you move into a threatening position? One where you could treat him/her in the same way? Hardly! Even in the remote case of such an unlikely outcome, what position would you then be in? Exactly! The same circumstances under which you now languish. So you may as well get used to doing this thing the right way. Get your boss promoted, or at least promotable, by helping his or her development. The second of the two nasty alternatives mentioned, above, is to "walk away." I mean, quite literally, that it is time to find other employment. In some really unimprovable situations, this is by far the best solution. Too many people, I find, spend large blocks of their life in some form of frustration related to the circumstance described here, doing neither one thing or the other. You must take action for your own sake, or you yourself are being immature.

This subject treatment, I hope, lends additional credence and import to my (Chapter Six) discussion on the critical nature of realistic job interviews and appraisals. If you allow yourself to be interviewed for a position without having opportunity to evaluate the organization "climate," or, as it is often referred to, "culture," with respect to maturity, you have failed yourself. You have also placed yourself at risk of being in an immature environment where structural vagaries and the excessive use of positional power limit the organization's development and your own personal growth and progress. While there is much you can do to bring about positive changes in the relatively mature setting, some organizations are much too far gone for you to engage in soul-destroying efforts against all odds. If you find yourself in such a setting, after careful appraisal of the chances for change, get out!

ORGANIZATION DEVELOPMENT THEORY

There is a large-scale programmatic change methodology for organizational improvement called Organization Development (OD). Some organizations even have OD specialists on their own staff, people whose assignment is to bring about wholesale maturation throughout all levels. There are consulting firms, also, who specialize in such organization change efforts. Results of these efforts, over the forty or so years of the history of OD, have been mixed. It is abundantly clear that two preconditions must exist for there to be a chance of much lasting change. The first condition is that every senior level executive must be fully committed to the program...so much so that they are individually willing to accept the possibility that they themselves are part of the current problems or difficulties being experienced. The second condition is even more demanding, for OD requires the commitment of very long periods of time. Results, if any, will be a very long time coming; in the process there may not be any tangible indication of progress for months, or years!

It is not hard to understand why many organizations are not able to meet these prerequisites, or why many who try OD abandon it in the early phases. I have a suggested reading or two on this subject, in the appendix.

THE NON-PROFIT ORGANIZATION

One of the reasons that bureaucratic forms of organization persist, particularly in the business sphere, is that goals of the tangible variety are easily identified and progress toward those goals measured. The ends, then, can very often justify the means, in fact the means can sometimes be ignored completely. This same "ends" focus, some argue, in extreme cases, is a <u>causative</u> factor in unethical practice.

Whether or not questionable practices are caused by a focus on specific goals is something I will not attempt to debate here, because I have a different purpose, a different relationship to show. An organization which focuses on tangible profits is rewarded, heavily in its own terms, by being <u>efficient</u>. Efficiency, in its simplest analysis, is some ratio of INPUTS over OUTPUTS. Efficiency can be measured by quantities of expenditure, resource commitment and utilization (INPUTS), or by some resultant, such as revenue or profit. For this reason, because such performances are so readily measured in absolute or relative terms, that is precisely what business organizations tend <u>to do</u>! They also tend, the few examples to the contrary acknowledged, spend less time considering the process, the <u>effectiveness</u> of their endeavors. Effectiveness is not nearly so readily identified, let alone measured! If all the automobile companies in the world are profitable, are they also effective? What of waste? What of Ecology? What of Societal benefit? What of Safety? What real progress has been made in <u>personal transportation</u>?

The relative successes achieved in pursuit of tangible goals and high levels of efficiency, unwittingly in many cases, precludes examination of the effectiveness questions of the grand scale. Not only that, but the system as a whole does not heavily reward (at least in the near term) those who may focus on effectiveness. The textbooks tell us that effectiveness is in meeting goals. I think that this is wrong, or only partly correct. Instead, I propose that an effective organization is one which can identify goals which balance the needs of all stakeholders, and then meet them consistently.

The problem of identifying goals with such broad impact is, of course, enormously challenging. Especially is this so when the international competition and other ferocious externalities are so significant in survival. It is an interesting test of one's values to ponder such a question as: "would you eat human flesh?" The circumstances, for most of us, would change our thresholds of acceptability for this behavior. Most, I contend, faced with death from starvation, would willingly eat the flesh of a dead human to sustain life. So it is with all values, or most. Choices are not easy, even if we have lofty ideals; and the lofty ideals in goal-setting for a complex organization are not very clear to anyone. Instead, the clear goals are indeed rather simple to define and so long as there are no obvious immoralities in their pursuit, the methods for reaching such goals become the focus of the managers attention.

Is it any wonder, then, that notions of "maturity" within organizational levels, and for individuals, even if understood, can be of secondary concern. The bureaucracy will attempt to define limits to power, and its application, in very precise terms. Inasmuch as one cannot define "creativity," the resultant bureaucratic form of organization is discouraging, perhaps even frustrating for the creative spirit. Ideas are strangled in such a system, or tend to be. The difference between a good profitable alternative and one which is a real breakthrough is a fine line indeed.

Another significant factor in the "business" or "for profit" entity, is the built-in connectedness (inter-dependency) of sub-units. This automatic tight-coupling between operating units almost demands control and efficiency. The purchasing department, for example, has prescriptions imposed by manufacturing, whose own limitations are often set by engineering. In an open system, the customers demands and those of financial reality dictate the product. All of this is a definition of a tightly coupled inter-dependency. When goals are defined, all sub-units can (theoretically) act in unison for goal attainment - because with efficient communications everyone understands what we are trying to achieve. Deviances are readily identified and appropriate actions (controls) taken. Again, the dominant factor in this form of success is <u>efficiency</u>. On the one hand, managing under such inter-dependent realities is a pleasure because of the structure, the definition, the controllability.

Now, by contrast, let's focus on the so-called "non-profit" organization, where several things make management a great deal more difficult. Here we find the conditions which make for surety of what we are trying to accomplish substantially missing, the methods of evaluation and control often vague and intangible. It is true that <u>any</u> organization can control costs and other resource utilization (INPUTS), but when the other side if the equation (OUTPUTS) are so vague and in some cases unmeasurable, how can we define an efficient cost ratio? The right amount to spend on a given venture or program becomes whatever any "expert" says it is. Then, later, we have no real method for verifying that expenditure. Similarly, in the extreme case, any program itself can be justified without meaningful reference to externalities. Even more damaging is the likelihood that programs and "products" will be developed without careful consideration of two things taken for granted by modern business entities. The first of these is whether or not "we" have the necessary strengths to do "it" very well; the second, is there a demand? In the "for profit" entity, taking on anything for which we have not developed unusual strength is an invitation to fail. Fail, that is, in terms of profits or finite returns to the shareholder.

Similarly, the real demand, or that which is or can be readily created, for a product or service is the other critical component in the strategic choice. We call this process, of course, matching strength with opportunity (or in some cases avoidance of threat). I am not claiming that in the non-profit sector we have no real ways of determining what the opportunities and threats are, merely that the inducements (economists might prefer the term <u>incentives</u>) are not so much in evidence and the methods for evaluating results are so much more obscure.

For all these reasons I have a hunch that people who gravitate toward non-profit organizations, and those who thrive in such, are substantially different from those who find the "business" challenge more exciting. What does this mean? Perhaps it means that we may not attain societal beneficiation which might occur if we could blend the philosophies (and process focus or effectiveness interests) of the not-for-profit with the strategic goal orientation of business. But I fear that without very specific and direct attempts to do so, Never the Twain Shall Meet.

Well, this may be the topic for another book, but for now let's consider what all this might mean for managers who wish to be effective, efficient and mature within a not-for-profit organization. If the reader has identified with my general definition of "loosely-coupled" organizations then there are some artificial means for building independency where none, or little, exists naturally, and, hence, in advancing maturity. Here are my suggestions, and I caution you that applying them is very difficult. You must remain constantly aware and strive to counter the negative effects of the following five realities:

1) Your organization is loosely-coupled. There are few inter-dependencies to help in the maturation process;

2) There will be almost complete focus, by everyone, on "process" and "means;" ends and outcomes may be ignored completely;

3) Internal criteria for prioritization will be invented;

4) When there is a crisis, of any kind, the organization will tend to become even more closed than usual;

5) The system, and top management, will resist all attempts to change the above four inevitabilities.

Unfortunately you will face many specific frustrations in your attempt to manage in a mature fashion. Some of the most important frustrations will come from the following:

1) Decisions will be made with illogical input sources (mismatches) and will lack clarity and focus;

2) The prioritization process, if any, will be inconsistent and will change for unclear reasons;

3) There will be little real followership, except that of the immature political kind;

4) There will substantial emphasis on "process;"

5) Criteria for decisions will not be in evidence;

6) Evaluations of all kinds will become vague or cease;

7) There will be scattering of efforts, inefficiency;

8) Even the good decisions will not be recognizable;

9) Who, What, Where and Why thinking is ignored;

10) The most mature people become discouraged first.

A glance at these lists might discourage anyone, but hang tough. Concentrate on the real meaning of maturity and make every effort to adhere to all of the edicts and other guidelines contained in these pages. Your overall objective, of course, is to inculcate high levels of mature followership. The way to this end, for you and your particular followers, is through acknowledgement of well-hidden interdependencies. A start in this can be made if you try to do the following five things especially religiously:

1 Acknowledge what is happening and why. Do not assume that it comes from stupidity or incompetence of top managers. . . the loosely-coupled system is virtually unmanageable;

2   Be especially open in your attempts to communicate. But make certain that you describe problems in non-personal ways; the immature will not tolerate criticism, nor will they comprehend your motives. Repeated attempts to communicate the same things over and over may be necessary. Remember that the framework for understanding is not nailed down;

3) Allow much more time than is reasonable for all forms of change to be accepted or ideas to be assimilated;

4) Find your rewards, if you can, on some high level of abstraction. Help others do likewise. Try to avoid unfocused criticism and especially avoid gossip;

5) Pay special attention to the politics of resources and go out of your way to acknowledge other people and what they do. Do not, however, expect reciprocal treatment;

6) Concentrate on higher-order objectives and consensus values. Remember, in the loosely coupled system if you do not anchor the values and repeatedly reset those anchors they will drift loose and be subject to spurious influences. If you cannot manage the culture (values especially) you can manage nothing!

If all this fails, buy a copy of this book for everyone in your organization and hold workshops, frequent discussions on the contents and the underlying ideas. Talk openly with everyone about what is happening and why. As you see progress being made, however slight, acknowledge it, praise it and nail it down!

In Chapter Ten I depart from management prescription and attempt the ambitious task of dealing with maturity in the largest and most complex organization: Global Society. There is much to be learned about maturity, and about the lack of it, in such an exercise.

CHAPTER 10

Global Maturity

This chapter is very different from all the others in this book. It seeks not to deliver edicts, guidelines or suggestions on how to become more mature as a manager, nor to divulge relevant theory which explains my position. Instead, it is a set of observations about a progression I see taking place in the world. A progression which I think is clearly related to maturity on the grand scale. People working in organizations represent a microcosm of the larger societal and global model.

All organizations, and indeed all individuals, are a part of a world-wide system; increasingly, the degree of acknowledged interdependence, or maturity, of peoples around the world plays a significant part in the performance of all organizations. In a remarkable and insightful book, The Borderless World, author Kenichi Ohmae refers to the "interlinking of economies" and discusses the enormous expansion of collaborative efforts and joint ventures which are currently spanning our ever-shrinking globe. These are very real manifestations of acknowledged interdependency on an international scale, but they are only part of the growing evidence of a maturing world. As with maturing individuals, of course, the world matures very slowly and exhibits regression, from time-to-time. Also, different parts of the world are at different stages of maturation and sometimes this progression is out-of-phase with economic progress.

The global model is a very useful one to examine; for in doing so, using my observations or your own, you will quickly realize just how slowly we make progress. It is my hope that this revelation will give you some comfort when you, or others in your own organization, seem to be painfully slow in attaining the levels of maturity you desire. Indeed in the global scene, in all smaller organizational models and in the individual, frequent and sustained regression is to be expected.

Let me suggest a few pieces of evidence for what might be indications of the overall global maturation phenomenon, though I'm certain that some readers might take issue with my interpretation of some of these. In the years since World War Two, virtually half-a-century, the only major military confrontations (Korea, Vietnam, Afghanistan and Iraq) have all ended without a clear-cut or final victor*. Throughout all human history, wars have been fought with victory as the objective and in the usual outcome the victor must vanquish, the defeated must be destroyed. Could it be that we have finally come to recognize the mature wisdom of cutting ones losses and walking away from an argument without "winning?" Or could it be that the notion of achieving certain ends but not necessarily the total destruction of another nation or its leaders has taken on some value different from those heretofore demonstrated? Insisting on having the "last word" is a sure sign of immaturity and it reflects a lack of understanding of anothers needs and rights, and a lack of appreciation for the interdependency of people everywhere.

As one might imagine, the writing of this book, and especially this chapter, has been a challenge because of the constant changes in the global scene. This particular section is added months after the chapter was "complete."

The reason for this addition is that, almost without prior warning, the Israeli's and the PLO have agreed to build an accord (this is late 1993). It is true that the basis of the accord is quite flimsy, and the future uncertain, but who would have thought that we would see Rabin and Arafat shaking hands on television screens all around the globe? Signs of a maturing world? I think maybe so.

At risk of oversimplifying the extraordinary turn of events in the Soviet block, beginning in 1989 and continuing as I write, I cannot help attaching my notion of maturity to these changes.

---

*   I realize that in the Gulf war, early in 1991, there was a clear-cut military victory. But the Allies, led by the USA, chose not to impose occupation, or oust Hussein.

The commitment to social, cultural and economic isolation by any one State, and with it the long held conviction that the whole world could be "converted" to a particular philosophy, have been replaced with acknowledged inter-dependencies, at least to an extent not previously witnessed. In an economic sense, this new position has placed enormous burdens upon the former Soviet (Unified States) peoples, because within their boundaries the immaturity of the economic systems and the inequities within and between the new independent states will cause (has already caused) massive dysfunction, even violent confrontation.

Nevertheless, I see these as signs of global "growing up." It has been eased, substantially, perhaps even accelerated, by an apparent willingness on the part of the other super-power (The USA) to do a little bit of growing-up itself. The posture of the United States in its dealings with the rest of the world has changed remarkably in these last few years. While there are still protectionists and other xenophobes, a growing majority of national leaders are acknowledging the true nature of our global inter-dependencies.

The situation in South Africa is similarly encouraging. As I write, various members of the two major groups of Black Peoples are still killing one-another, but at long last we see real commitment to a major and permanent reversal of Apartheid - elections involving all citizens are imminent.

It is a curious thing about collective and individual rebellion; it is more likely to be manifest AFTER some reduction in repression, rather than during periods of extreme repression. This confirms, it seems to me, the theory of transcendence - people become independent, in the extreme, after a long or powerfully felt period of enforced dependency. This was certainly true in the case of the American Civil rights Movement of the 1960's, as it is in South Africa today. Extremism in expressing independence, though fully understandable, serves to delay maturation and the move toward acknowledged interdependence. This is true in individuals, in organizations and in whole nations.

The August/September (1990) accords of the United Nations in their attempts to deal with the Iraqi invasion of Kuwait seem to be further evidence of world maturity. Even if these accords did not produce entirely desirable outcomes, and even if some nations seemed to lose their resolve, it still remains a rather strong and encouraging indication of a maturing world. It is true that UN progress at this time is, in part, a reflection that the USSR veto is gone and the Chinese influence suspended, but there is an encouraging new level of relative agreement at the UN.

Another item of a global nature, in my list of evidences for world maturity, transcends human interaction into the critical area of acknowledging inter-dependencies with all non-human aspects of our planet, and beyond. I refer, of course, to the environmental movement. Though there have been several prior periods in which it seemed that an awakening was taking place, this time that form of change seems to have some global impetus. As with the South African situation, progress is painfully slow; and as with South Africa, those with strong commitments to their cause (zealots) become impatient, and quite immature in their attempts to push the movement faster, and in extreme cases in clearly wrong headed directions. There is also the obvious, and obviously regressive, political ramifications and just where this particular movement will take us seems a little uncertain. But in terms of a general progression toward greater maturity it is encouraging and the progress we might make will come not one moment too soon.

The final item, one which is unwinding as I write, is one taking place in the American movement called "Diversity" (and I understand similar movements exist in Europe and in other parts of the world). This, too, has some very quirky aspects, but led by intellectuals in academe, there are serious attempts being made at inclusiveness. Attempts to ensure not just that all individuals, regardless of ethnicity, gender, etc., are given equal opportunity, but also that the very contributions of literature, the arts, philosophy and other academic subjects and research from around the globe are included, embraced and valued, along with more traditional "Western" contributions and values.

This last one has, in fact, stirred up quite a controversy, being labeled "politically correct." The controversy stems from the fact that some with political agendae have seized the occasion to bring about acceptance of truly bizarre ideas and dogma. This is transparent to all but those who are equally immature in their opposition - the intransigent, that is. Nevertheless, even these contrasting groups, and all those somewhere on middle ground are finding more open ways to debate their differences. Interesting to me is the fact that it was

Aristotle who urged rejection of extremism; and Plato who urged that women, as well as men, have the ability and wisdom to lead societies. Great ideas are timeless, it seems.

In all these situations there are factors propelling the moves toward maturity, though not always are altruistic factors dominant or even present. But such is the case for all forms of maturation, individual or otherwise. There is nothing quite so likely to propel one from a state of independence to a more "acknowledging of others" state, one of mature interdependency, than the realization that our independence can be self-destructive! Even the most disadvantaged (nation, group or individual) has much to gain from a gradual progression toward inter-dependency, perhaps, in fact. The most disadvantaged have the most to gain. Sixty years ago, Gandhi seemed to understand this. Faced with deplorable conditions and military oppression, he advocated not just passivism, but deliberate non-violent interaction.

THE NEGATIVE SIGNS

I hastily acknowledge that the news is not all good, though it might be seen as encouraging. In many parts of the world, still, there are serious intercultural conflicts as various groups seek to assert their rights and claim their "place at the table." If you examine all of these situations carefully, there is fundamental evidence of the inevitable progression: dependence, independence, and interdependence. In addition to the structural barriers to this progression, however, there are still some powerful social impediments to the maturation process. As always, great cultural rifts and immature reluctance to acknowledge interdependence are at the root of all such conflicts and a slow change in this posture brings about gradual change. But let me identify some other reasons for the retardation of the global maturation process, some of the most compelling "negative" factors.

Human Recycling

Assume that the average "mature" individual has somewhere in the neighborhood of thirty years of significant influence. By this I mean that after going through ones own maturation processes and before going into physical and/or mental decline, we might, with luck, have thirty years of high influence potential. During that time, the extent of the influence is limited by changes in the environment and in members of the succeeding generation (social change). Inter-generational influence was at its greatest level when the rate of change was relatively slow. These days, even in the very conservative socie-ty of Japan, the degree to which the younger generation of Japanese venerate the ways and advice of their elders is decreasing. In Ameri-ca, where the rate of change has been more noticeable for some time, the "Generation Gap" has long existed and has long limited the trans-fer of "wisdom" between generations. To go back to the concept of "assigned" power (Chapter Four), we see that succeeding generations are less willing, in the Western world, to assign much power to the older generations. This factor (human recycling) is undoubtedly a major explanation for why we (humankind) have not demonstrated strong abilities to learn from our own history. That disability, or break-down in communication channels, is in some ways intensified by the rapid rate of change in mores, standards and conventions within any one nation or other social organization. Major religious groups, with their well articulated covenants and creeds, tend to serve as a damper to this negative progression, but for many religions their strength and their resolve has diminished somewhat, under social pressures.

Social Upheaval

One of the many ways in which our society has changed is seen in the level of interactivity (and interdependency) among family members; it has definitely decreased in the economically advanced nations. The notion of a "nuclear family," with significant and pro-longed contact between three or more generations, has been replaced by national and global scattering of family members. I make no value judgments about this, but do claim that it serves to inculcate a sense of independence by family members. As an American immigrant from Europe, I know that I severed the potential influences by grand-parents, parents and older siblings, for both myself and my wife, when I left my homeland at age twenty-two. Increasingly, and not

just in America, populations are made up of ever increasing proportions of nomadic individuals or "incomplete" families. Some would
argue that these changes are positive, and certainly those who hold the
value of <u>independence</u> sacred would do so. I merely point out that
these aspects of familial interdependence are on the decline, globally.
To the degree that this change induces and sustains <u>independence</u>, it
also limits progression toward MATURITY through <u>acknowledged</u>
<u>inter-dependencies</u>.

Liberal Thinking (and overcompensation)

In one sense, liberal thinking seems to be a real assist to the
notion of interdependency. There is an automatic assumption in
liberal philosophy that people need help from each other and from the
system, and there is plenty of evidence that some indeed do. On the
other hand, built into the transcendence model, introduced in Chapter
Three, is the reality that interdependency can only come to those who
first experience the progression from dependence through independence to inter-dependent maturity. This, I acknowledge, gives us a
bleak prognosis for society; the less fortunate among us may NEVER
have the experience of multi-faceted independence. Instead, they
may, as a results of well-intentioned legislation and other "helping"
activity, be relegated to a near permanent state of dependence. It is
this aspect of the liberal versus conservative argument which gives
rise to the (false) notion that conservatives are heartless. It presumes
that the best solution for the unfortunate is to provide FOR THEM,
rather than provide opportunities for genuine growth through individual efforts. As Winston Churchill said "If you are not a liberal when
you are young, you have no heart.... if you are not a conservative
when you are older, you have no head." The acknowledgement of
transcendent maturity is implicit in Sir Winston's remark. These
arguments, and indeed the "conflict of visions" reality (Thomas
Sowell) are behind the major philosophical clashes between these two
ideologies. I wonder if we may ever reach a place where, in maturity,
opponents on these and related philosophies and political dimensions
can compromise?

As a kind of aside, and while discussing politics, in 1990 a new
political movement or philosophy emerged in America, it is labeled
the "Communitarian Movement." Prominent intellectuals such as

Sociologist Amitai Etzioni are leading this movement whose central mission sounds a lot like a commitment to <u>interdependency</u>. It is based, however, on a frontal assault on individualism, so it may well find significant resistance in this country. Individualism which is mature, which has <u>transcended</u> independence of thought and action, does not ignore the value of interdependency. The Communitarian movement, with all the best intentions, may fail politically for this reason alone. In any event, it is in its infancy and the old-line political parties are solidly entrenched. While they (the traditional political parties in America) may indeed be part of the problem, they are in a remarkably strong position to resist, in a very immature fashion, emerging new socio-economic theories and movements.

There is another way in which, innocently enough, liberal thinking impedes large scale transference of wisdom; it encourages and embraces change, sometimes for its own sake. To the degree that conservative approaches hold traditions, they also increase the likelihood of intergenerational learning. I make no claim that this is all good, merely the one point stressed. I also acknowledge that change itself, and under the right circumstances, has the potential to induce valuable new learning.

I owe sincere apologies to adherents of liberal and conservative beliefs, and probably to those involved in the Communitarian movement. In no way are the above comments sufficiently broad or deep to approach explanation or elucidation. My reason for mentioning these very narrow aspects of the two opposing political points of view is to show that organizational challenges are not very far removed from the on-going national and international challenges they mirror. Sometimes we forget, in the everyday "battles" of management, that our organization is but a socio-cultural entity not unlike (though in most cases substantially less complex) that of a nation-state. The "glue" which holds any such entity together depends, of course, on the nature of the fabric. In turn, one of the most critical determinants of the nature of the fabric is the collective maturity. Just as with individuals, who, as they mature tend to have days and acts which are less mature than others, progress being spastic, so it is with collectives. Organizations (and organizational leaders), societies (and societal leaders) must learn to understand the realities of such setbacks and their significance. The benefits which can accrue to a MATURE individual also apply to the whole of society and to sub-units of it, such as your organization.   .

A FINAL COMMENT

There has been a long and constant progression of understanding on the incredibly complex phenomenon we call "organization" for many decades now. Despite the progress, however, many important questions remain unanswered still. I thumbed through a book which I treasure and found the following passage:

> The art of human collaboration seems to have disappeared. . . The various nations seem to have lost all capacity for international cooperation in the necessary tasks of civilization. The internal condition of each nation is not greatly better: it seems that only a threat from without, an unmistakable emergency, can momentarily quiet the struggle of rival groups. . . How can humanity's capacity for spontaneous co-operation be restored? It is in this area that leadership is most required. . . a type of knowledge that has escaped us in two hundred years of prosperous development. How to substitute human responsibility for strife and hatreds - this is one of the most important researches of our time.

These words were written, as part of a preface to a book, by the remarkable Elton Mayo, in 1939. The book was Management and the Worker by Roethlisberger and Dixon. It documents the research done by the Harvard School of Business research team at the Hawthorne Plant of Western Electric Company, in the 1920's. Most management scholars would acknowledge that these studies form the foundation for all modern and behaviorally based management understandings, not because of the answers they provided, but through the questions raised.

It is my hope that Management Maturity, can add just a tiny grain of weight to our progress, a little more to our collective commitment to the acknowledgement of our interdependency and a partial answer to Dr. Mayo's crucial and still relevant question.

APPENDIX A

References and Recommended Readings

At the end of any book, especially one which intends to be prescriptive, or instructive, there should be a statement about the inherent limitations. This book certainly is not a comprehensive coverage of all that is known about management, leadership, organization behavior, communications and the several other topics I have so ambitiously attempted. As a matter of fact, my purpose is quite the opposite, to exclude the vast majority of information on any of these subjects. There are gains to be made, and some obvious losses, by taking this approach. First, the whole thing becomes manageable! One of the things I try to teach inexperienced managers is that the first thing one must learn, in any position in life, especially in management, is just exactly what one can reasonably accomplish. To spend time either trying to accomplish everything, or fretting about the fact that one can't, is utter foolishness. It is with that spirit that I drew a line around the component parts of this modest little book and proscribed the extent (breadth and depth) to which I would go in each section, on each subject. As an academic exercise, then, it would fail, for that reason alone. As a tool for practitioners, with the widest possible audience in mind, this constriction, I hope, makes much more sense. And even for the narrower audience, those with purely academic interest I have, I think, provided a glimpse of how some theory can be directly related to real-world applications and, in the materials of this appendix, identified some trailheads for the discovery of more extensive information.

The second gain in my approach to the boundaries of this book is that simply by restricting the <u>amount</u> of information I have the greatest possible chance that people will actually read and understand what I say. It is one thing for an academic to insist that students (trapped in the reality of pass/fail and grades, etc.) read everything on a given subject, quite another to be so presumptuous about busy readers who have other things to occupy their time and consciousness.

A third gain is that I can exclude topics which, though they may have value, are not (either) very prescriptive or not supportive of prescription, or are not essential in developing a worthwhile growth in management maturity. After all, my objective is in building an appreciation for, perhaps a commitment to, the maturation process and its advantages (as defined here). My objective is nothing more than that.

Given the limitations, then, I have a responsibility to those readers who might want to go a little further on some, or maybe all of, the topics broached in my manuscript. For this reason I offer, in the pages following this one, not the usual sterile reference list, but an expanded or annotated one. It too is severely restricted. One of the things anyone discovers when following an information trail is that the more you come to discover, the more you realize how little you know, and how vast the available information base. This, in fact, is the great paradox of advanced education! I hope that those who follow the trails identified below will benefit, as I have, by exploring the works of <u>just a few</u> of the great minds behind the literature, theory and information on management.

Another point which must be stressed here, again, is the deliberate exclusion of what I refer to as the many "fads," or fashions of management emphasis. Those of you in the business world, and other spheres perhaps, will know exactly what I mean by this...the current fad seems to be the emphasis on "QUALITY," or total quality(TQM). There is no doubt that one of the several keys to America's industrial future is the notion that we can/must produce products and services of quality. The problem is (see my comments about slogans, etc., on page 49) that without high levels of commitment by a high percentage of the workforce, quality will always be temporary, forced, or illusory. Quality of ideas, of products and services comes from the maturity of the processes. In turn, the maturity of the process can only come from the enthusiastic commitment of people on every level!

REFERENCES and Recommended Reading

Presented in order of appearance and using either author name, title of the work or subject matter, as in the book.

The One-Minute Manager, by Ken Blanchard and Spencer Johnson (William Morrow Publishers, 1982) was a roaring success in sales, several million copies! While it cannot be read in "one minute" (it actually takes an hour or so) it is/was a useful item for all managers to read. There's some fundamental wisdom in the prescriptions; the premise, however, is rather narrow. The many sequels add significantly.

In Search of Excellence, by Tom Peters and Bob Waterman, was also a giant success (publishers: Warner Books, 1982). This book was based on the identification, by the authors, of America's "best-run" companies and the common elements among them which seem to produce "excellence." While this is an informative prescription it is aimed at the organization as an entity, rather than offering specific guidelines for managers as individuals (with the few notable exceptions I refer to in these pages). I do recommend it to senior managers, as I do the sequel, A Passion for Excellence, published by Random House (1985).

Herb Simon is a special case for inclusion here. The reference to "bounded rationality" (p.2) in the decision process is certainly one of the things for which Professor Simon is best known. But for all those people who want to study management intensively, I recommend all of the works of this man. He is a true genius; one of the few people, ever, to have earned the rank of Full Professor in three different disciplines: Economics; Management; and (relatively recently) Computer Science. I especially recommend, in connection with the contents of this book, "Rational Decision Making in Business Organizations." This article was published in the American Economic Review, September, 1979.

Fred Herzberg, behavioral scientist, is a central figure in the "behavioral school" of management. Herzberg is a highly prolific researcher but, perhaps, is best known for what has been labeled the "two-factor" theory of motivation. His conclusions came from a series of intensive studies of professionals in the workplace. Managers everywhere should read the report in one of its forms (it was published in a variety of media). The best bet, in my view: the 1966 book titled Work and the Nature of Man; World Publishing Company. A prescriptive outcome of Herzberg's conclusions about motivation also is a very worthwhile read. This appeared in the Harvard Business Review in 1968 and was titled "One More Time; How Do You Motivate Employees." These are classic, there's no doubt; but (at risk of being self-serving) the Herzbergian (and other) notions of intrinsic motivation miss an important factor: the MATURITY of the workers and the manager, as dealt with here.

Abraham Maslow, regarded by many as the father of the humanistic school of psychology*; he is certainly a major contributor to the founding of the behavioral school of management. His theories on intrinsic motivation, particularly his "hierarchy of needs" have been often criticized, by a few even ridiculed, but they are still taught as ways of conceptualizing the drives behind human behavior of all kinds. The essence of Maslow is presented in the pages of this book, but I recommend to readers, also, "Eupsychian Management", published by Richard D. Irwin, Inc. in 1965. In a foreword by Warren Bennis (himself a leadership scholar of considerable renown) there is reference to the unpronounceable title of Maslow's book. Bennis says, and I agree, that readers should not be "scared off" by the title. It may well be that none of Maslow's theories can/will ever be proven or disproven. This does not take away the value of this man's work in helping conceptualize some very fundamental realities of human behavior. If nothing else, the Maslow Need Hierarchy is a spectacularly successful heuristic device!

On Mentoring. Surprisingly little empirical research has been done on this subject (by comparison with many other management-related topics), especially considering its ancient origins. For readers who wish to go further in understanding what is known of mentoring,

---

*   In order to gain a better, or more comprehensive, view of human behavioral principles and conflicting theories, one should read the founding contributions of the behavioral school (Skinner and Watson, especially) and the cognate school (Freud and others) - in basic books on psychological principles.

I recommend as a starting place the work of Rosabeth Kanter. Professor Kanter has recently served as editor of the Harvard Business
Review and so may have moved beyond the focused study of mentoring, but her work on mentoring is particularly strong. For a treatment slightly less academic, more directly usable, I suggest the delightful little book Mentor Relationships: How They Aid Creative
Achievement, Endure, Change and Die, by E. Paul Torrance, Bearly
Publishing, (1984).

The Hawthorne Studies, undoubtedly the foundation stone for
the modern management era, are fully documented in a remarkable
publication Management and the Worker by Roethlisberger and
Dickson - Harvard University Press (1939). Obviously this classic is
no longer in print, but university libraries everywhere (particularly
where there is a school of business) will have a copy. You may find
this an exciting pathway to the realization of how the workplace has
changed in the last several decades - and also an appreciation for the
considerable complexities which challenge anyone who wishes to
conduct meaningful research in organizations. This is a true classic!

Chris Argyris has been one of the most prolific academic writers
on the subject of human behavior, in general, and workplace motivations in particular. The Argyris model of maturation presented here is
but one of many of his contributions. Among the more than 200
publications from this distinguished gentleman it is hard to select just
one, but try The Individual and Organization: Some problems of
Mutual Adjustment, published, originally, in Administrative Science
Quarterly (June, 1957).

While on the subject of MATURITY, the maturity model which
forms the basis for this book has many foundations. The original
conceptualization comes from J. W. Pfeiffer & J. E. Jones who used
it, originally, in group counseling and facilitation. Walt Boshear and
Karl Albrecht then adapted the concept for inclusion in a delightful set
of descriptive models called Understanding People; Models and Concepts. This is now out of print, I'm told, but you may find a copy in
your local academic library. The publisher was University Associates, Inc. (1977).

Cultures, as a study within management, is a relatively recent inclusion. Certainly within the last decade there has been growing awareness that this dimension of human "grouping" is quite meaningful in explaining, among other things, "within culture" cohesion. It is also useful in identifying problems at the intercultural interfaces, both inside and at the boundaries of the organization itself. On the subject of corporate culture, I like, particularly, the work of Terry Deal, and of Edgar Schein. See Deal's Corporate Cultures: The Rites and Rituals of Corporate Life (Addison Wesley, 1982), and Schein's Organizational Culture and Leadership (Jossey-Bass, 1985). On the subject of intercultural problems within organization not much has been developed yet*. The best bet is to study group theory and related subjects. A good place to start such study would be with Marvin Shaw's Group Dynamics: The Psychology of Small Group Behavior, McGraw-Hill (1971). Also see Organizational Socialization & Group Development" in The Academy of Management Review (October, 1984); and "Interorganizational Groups; Origins, Structure, Outcomes" in The Academy of Management Review (October, 1987).

Conflict and its resolution, like the subject of cultures, has many dimensions. I recommend readers start with L. David Brown's "Managing Conflict Among Groups" in Organizational Psychology: A Book of Readings, Prentice-Hall (1979). I particularly like Eric Nielsen's "Understanding & Managing Intergroup Conflict" in Managing Group & Intergroup Relations, Irwin - Dorsey Press (1972). There is also a very strong section on this subject in James Thompson's classic Organizations in Action (McGraw-Hill, 1967).

Bureaucracy, or at least the formal and academic study of it, has its origins with Max Weber, and there are only two translations of Weber's original work. Both are classic and likely to be in any major library, but these are rather heavy going for most people. Two modern scholars on the subject who should be studied are Charles Perrow and Peter Blau. Perrow's Complex Organizations; A Critical

---

* I believe that there is room for academics to develop a line of research in this
   area. . . the "other" kind of culture, corporate culture, has received most
   attention.

Essay was published by Scott, Foresman & Co. (1979) and Blau's
The Dynamics of Bureaucracy was published by The University of
Chicago Press (1973). Both of these authors have published substan-
tial materials on this subject, and many others.

The Larry Greiner model of organizational change, labelled
"The Evolution - Revolution" model, I find particularly compelling.
Readers can find discussion of it in any good Organization Theory
text, or find a copy of The Harvard Business Review, July/August,
1972. The article is titled "Evolution and Revolution as Organizations Grow." It's as good a depiction of the ways in which organizations change with time and circumstances as any you will find.

Power, and particularly the bases of power in organizations, is
analyzed in detail by French and Raven in "The Bases of Social
Power" in a section of Studies in Social Power, published in 1959 by
the Institute for Social Research. Though this is not terribly accessi-
ble to most people, it must be acknowledged for spawning much of
the more recent research in this area. The best discussion, and expansion, of the French and Raven notions I have found in a textbook:
Richard Hodgett's Organization Behavior: Theory and Practice,
published by McMillan in 1991.

Frustration is a subject rarely dealt with in management literature, at least under that name. It is implicit, however, in the subject
of stress, which is commonly discussed in more applied management
literature*. One of the early, and still very valuable treatments of this
subject (stress) is in R.L. Kahn, et al., Organizational Stress, published by Wiley(1964).
A more general coverage of stress, and certainly more recent, is
in the Handbook of Industrial and Organizational Psychology (Rand
McNally, 1978).... the chapter by Joseph E. McGrath, "Stress and
Behavior in Organizations". There is a useful article in Personnel
Psychology (Spring, 1979), titled "Personal and Organizational Strategies for Handling Job Stress." Many people, I find, have a strange

*   The problem with examining literature on stress as a way of coming to understand
     frustration is that stress is not the same thing as frustration. But frustration
     may be a form of stress that has been neglected by management researchers.
     Another possible line of research?

notion of what stress is. It is not what someone, or some situation, does to or imposes upon an individual. Instead, it is the response, bodily, internally, psychological and biological, to externalities. What one person finds stressful another may not! For the original information, and still by far the most informative, see the classic by Hans Selye The Stress of Life, published by McGraw-Hill in 1956, and again in 1976.

Communications is such a huge topic; on its own it fills many books, of course. I do recommend that readers try Marshall McLuhan's classic Understanding Media: The extensions of Man, though it is heavy going for some and is rather philosophical. Nevertheless it grounds all useful questions about communications. There is a very enlightning examination of semantics, and similar problems of miscommunications in S.I. Hayakawa's Language in Thought and Action published by Harcourt Brace Jovanovitch (1949). Some aspects of informal communications problems are covered very well in Rumor and Gossip: The Social Psychology of Hearsay published by Elsevier Press (1976). For a more comprehensive treatment of communications, see D.K. Benlo's The Process of Communications, publisher: Holt, Rinehart & Winston (1960). For the "nuts and bolts" of writing memo's, letters, holding meetings, etc., there's a host of useful books on the shelves of your local bookstore. Many of these have some value, though most are devoid of theory and very narrow.

MBO, or Management by Objectives, is, in one form or another, in wide usage in large organizations and institutions. Also, virtually any textbook on management will have a section devoted to the subject. The observations and recommendations in this book (on MBO) are somewhat "out of the mainstream." For a traditional approach to the subject, see Managing By Objectives, by Anthony P. Raya - Scott, Foresman, publisher (1974). The original work on this is from Peter Drucker (The Practice of Management, Harper and Row, 1954). For a short, yet very valuable, discussion of MBO which matches my conception, see "Some Modifications of MBO as an OD Strategy", by Steven Kerr in Organization Development; Progress and Perspectives, Robey and Altman, McMillan Publishing Co. (1982).

There are a couple of references to Japanese Management in my book. I am not really sure that there exists any such thing, but nevertheless it is a common expression. Any attempt to come to terms with what this might mean, in my opinion, should start with William Ouchi's Theory Z: How America Can Meet the Japanese Challenge, published by Addison Wesley in 1981. A really first-class synopsis exists in (Ch.15) of Andrew DuBin's Contemporary Applied Management, Business Publications Inc. (1985). While there are some recent revelations about Japanese business practices which are not discussed in these works, they do provide a good foundation for further study.

On the subject of Planning and Strategy, and the closely related sub-topics of efficiency and effectiveness there are plenty of good sources. The finest available, however, is in a very recent textbook The Strategy Process by Henry Mintzberg and James Brian O'Quinn. The publisher is Prentice-Hall (1991).

Katz and Kahn's The Social Psychology of Organizations, published by Wiley in 1978, will provide readers with much in-depth information on many of the topics of my book. It is especially useful, I find, in developing an appreciation for the complexities of the organization as a SYSTEM.

On Leadership, per se, there is probably more information in print than any other management topic. It is therefore difficult to select. . . especially since leadership is really all about the skillful application of virtually all the other topics in management. Of the greatest influence to me (as a manager, as an educator, and in trying to identify a meaningful and workable set of information for this book) has been Hersey and Blanchard's Situational Leadership. You will find abundant references to their model in articles and books, but the one I would recommend is in the Training and Management Journal of February 1974. It is titled "So You Want To Know Your Leadership Style?" The original place for the H-B situational leadership prescription was in Stogdill and Coon's (1957) Book Leader Behavior: Description and Measurement, though it (the model) has gone through some revision in the intervening years. The major revision was in adding the maturity dimension. As I point out in the pages of this book, I believe that the concept of maturation as it re-

lates to the workplace needs even further revision to include the
ACKNOWLEDGEMENT OF INTER-DEPENDENCY!

The reference to Machiavelli, in Chapter 9, is an acknowledgement, at least, that politics is a fundamental reality in organizations.
It is more, however, and I am fully aware that some will accuse me of
"reaching" to suggest that "mature" people do not indulge in practices
Machiavelli would label as natural, the self-serving behaviors we see
all around us. I'll take that criticism and certainly urge readers to
examine what Machiavelli had to say, and what Freud had to say.
One nice (convenient) way to examine Machiavelli in the management
context, is through the eyes of Anthony Jay. Jay wrote a little gem
called Management and Machiavelli, published by Bantam Books in
1978. Any introductory work in Psychology will introduce the basic
Freudian assumptions about personality. But also, I must urge, take a
look at what Plato had to say and, especially, Jean Jacques Rousseau,
on the subject of compassion and benevolence. In other words, there
are many views of humanity, not just those of the cynics.

There are a couple of references, in these pages, to loosely-
coupled systems. Though the original conceptualization of this is
difficult to pin down, there is no doubt that the clearest attempt to
define the significance of loose-coupling is by Carl Weick ("Educa-
tional Organizations as Loosely Coupled Systems" in Administrative
Science Quartery March, 1976). For a complex analysis of loose-
coupling and its relationship to the subjects of interdependence/auton-
omy within complex organizations, see (Ch.4 of) Howard Aldrich's
classic Organizations and Environments, Prentice-Hall, 1979.

On the subject of Managing Upward, or managing one's own
boss, there is a fine treatment in Organization and People by J.B.
Richie and Paul Thompson, West Publishing, 1988.

Organization Development is a huge subject all of its own. For
a comprehensive review of what it is and how it is applied, there is no
finer single source than French and Bell's Organization Development,
published by Prentice-Hall in 1978. For a series of publications, each
on a different sub-topic of OD, the Addison Wesley Series, various
authors and various publication dates, provides concise little mono-
graphs which are excellent.

Much of the modern research on management and organizations has origins in the foregoing materials. As we (academics) progress in our understanding of this highly complex subject, we tend to focus, more and more, on some very narrow aspect of research. Regrettably, few are taking the more holistic approach or in other ways are tying together the little bits of information we gather. Many of the works cited in the preceding pages have the kinds of approach I feel we lack. They may, in some cases, not reflect the most recent of findings. . . they do in my opinion, however, provide excellent grounding for anyone who wants to go further in developing their own foundations and advanced understanding of the body of theory related to management. Or perhaps might serve those who wish to build a base from which to do current research on the more narrow topics.

APPENDIX B

A Case Study in Management Maturity

     The following story has been written to illustrate some of the dysfunctions organizations can, and often do, experience. It therefore provides an opportunity for readers of <u>Management Maturity</u> to consider the application of many of the concepts and edicts found in the book to real-life situations. It is hoped that, in so doing, a better understanding will develop of the Maturity concept; but also that these exercises will stimulate thoughts about how to apply this understanding to other working situations and particularly to a reader's own environments. The Case is entirely fictitional and any similarities between characters or situations in any "real world" organization is purely coincidental. While a merger is significant in the story, the situations which have arisen and the difficulties identified could just as easily occur in any organization. The merger merely accentuates problems of immaturity and, especially, problems at sub-unit interfaces.

     The Case story is followed by an analytic conversation which includes some direct prescriptions based on the practical edicts and theory contained in the foregoing pages. The contrived "conversation" is between myself and a student. The case was originally written as a final examination in Organization Theory. The student, Joan Pedersen, answered the case so well that I decided to modify some of her observations creating this dialog. Her side of the conversation is made up of comments and questions which are typical of someone studying management in the academic way. In other words she uses what I would consider to be the "normal" academic analysis mode, using theories of management, organization and organization behavior as taught in business/management programs. There is emphasis in this conversation on describing what is going on in theoretical terms. Any prescription may be found in my comments, or "replies."

GEORGE AND THE FRANKLIN CHEMICAL COMPANY;
A Case Study

George was not feeling great about his life as he climbed aboard the commuter train, headed for his home in the Baltimore suburbs, and he found himself thinking very negatively about the last several days. His old colleague and friend, Mary Wilson, had been fired for not complying with some of the new company policies; his own department budget had been cut (again); he had been told by his own boss, Marketing Vice-president Art Pepper, to "Get with the program George, this company is moving fast and we need your 100% commitment!"

Earlier in the week he had been shocked to hear from one of his Texas sales managers that three long-term accounts, old friends of George's former boss Harold Thompson, had advised that they were switching to another supplier. The reason they had all given was that they had found an alternative source for all their chemical needs. This had been particularly galling to George because he had fought Pepper for days over the top management decision to halt Texas production on two large volume products which were critical to his customers in the Southwestern petrochemical industries. George had known better than to call Pepper with that "I told you so!" message, but he had felt so angry and so frustrated. Pepper's retort that "there are other fish to fry, George, so get your people cranked up and find new business on our more profitable products," had made him feel much worse.

There had been a time in George's career when he literally lived for his work and put in endless hours with great enjoyment, at a far lower salary than he now earned. Only five years prior to this time George had received his first big management break, being made sales manager for the old Thompson company. During the two years which followed that promotion George had felt he was right in the middle of all the Thompson planning and key decision making, and he had felt especially close to the entire management team and to the old man, Harold Thompson. There were so many positive aspects to his work, then, and though the company had never really met its goals for sales and profits, and the competition had been ferocious, he had really felt terrific.

George reflected on the take-over by Franklin Chemicals and realized that despite the personal progress he had made in the three years since the merger, he still did not feel as though he "fit." "Maybe it's Baltimore," he thought, but he really could not be sure that this was true... his wife and children had adapted extremely well to life in Maryland! They had made new friends, had a new and beautiful house, a 36 foot boat which they sailed on the Chesapeake. "Why am I not happy?" George asked himself, "What the heck is wrong with me?"

Franklin Chemicals is a twenty-year-old company which manufactures a wide variety of chemicals and supplies for industrial applications. Arthur Franklin, the dynamic founder and chairman of the company, is a former chemical engineer who had been very creative when on the Dupont staff, in the 1960's. He had purchased a couple of small chemical manufacturing companies to form the Franklin company in 1970 and had personally been the driving force behind a tremendously successful growth period. By 1983 Franklin Chemicals had come to be recognized as a very tightly controlled and efficient regional company which dominated certain markets of the Eastern Seaboard. In 1985 the company had "gone public," with Franklin remaining as the Chairman but with a new President, Joan Cole, as "the much needed professional manager" - to quote the annual report of that year.

Cole had been most aggressive in her internal restructuring of the company, then in 1989, after a couple of very strong profit performances, had moved to acquire two other regional companies in the same industry, in a bold attempt to "go national." One of the ac-

quired companies was in Texas (Thompson Co.) and one in California. These acquisitions had more than doubled the size of the new
national company and had thrust the organization into great visibility
in the industry and the stock market. In the months following the
mergers Franklin had continued to grow rapidly in spite of some
awful internal problems, resulting in: decisions made to unify certain
products; unification of operating policies/procedures and the creation
of an amalgamated management structure; and very significant employee turnover.

George had worked for the Dallas-based Thompson company
since graduating from SMU with his MBA. He had started as an
inside market analyst, then out in a sales territory for a while; then
had received the promotion to sales manager. Old man Thompson
had been a joy to work with. Yes, there had been a few problems and
difficulties, but somehow this management team had found a way to
survive and had made reasonable profits, in which they all shared.
When Franklin bought out Thompson, the "old man" took the money
for his stock and retired. The management team had participated in a
stock option plan and so received cash for their shares. George had
invested in a new house with his proceeds. When Mr. Thompson
retired he had held a huge Texas barbecue on his ranch, for all the
employees, and everyone at the party expressed their concerns about
the new organization. Most of the managers were actually quite
optimistic, the reputation of the Franklin company being so excellent.

As the commuter train slowed in its approach to the Glen Burnie
railroad station, George found himself daydreaming a little, reminisc-
ing about that farewell party for "H.T." He remembered thinking
how incredible it was that so many customers, suppliers, local officials and just plain friends had been in attendance. He could see,
still, the huge hind of beef on the rotisserie, could smell it, and could
feel the warmth of the hot coals on his face, and the warmth, too, of
the many friendships evident at that party. He then realized, a little
sheepishly, that he was actually shedding a tear. He quickly wiped
his eye, and stood up to collect his brief-case and coat from the
overhead rack as the train came to a halt.

George located his car and slipped behind the wheel, ready for
his ten-minute drive home. He found himself, again, thinking of his

time with Thompson. This was, he knew, quite inappropriate. His current problems and challenges were screaming for his attention and here he was, more threatened than ever, thinking about the past. But he couldn't seem to help it! There was such a sense of direction at the old company, and a solid understanding, by everyone it seemed, of just what Thompson was trying to accomplish. Relationships with suppliers and customers were extremely close, and the development of new products always seemed to be based on collaborative efforts among insiders, suppliers and customers. George knew that some of the products had not been particularly profitable, but the "old man" had told everyone, "Look, we stay alive by ascertaining that our relationships with customers are sustained. We make sure that they can meet their goals using our products, and they remain loyal to us." It certainly seemed to be true; George couldn't remember ever losing an account of any real size. Until now, that is! "Maybe I'm just incompetent" he said to himself, "maybe in the old days, H.T. was just carrying me with his own enthusiasm." He didn't really believe that, but. . .

It had been quite a blow to everyone at Thompson when "H.T." told all the employees of the buy-out offer from Franklin and his decision to take it. Once that announcement had been made, it had seemed almost immediate that the transaction was completed. George had thought it extremely odd that during the take-over no-one from Franklin had talked to him, or to any of the other managers. For a while, however, after the merger, there were no real changes. . . the grapevine had it that the "big bosses" were pretty busy settling some real problems in the new California company. One of the earliest changes was in having all the Dallas vice-presidents report to the president, in Baltimore. These three had all been good friends of George and one, the vice-president of marketing, had been his immediate boss. George felt, at that point, a noticeable slowdown in decisionmaking, and several times during this period he had gone ahead and made decisions that he thought appropriate only, later, to be really criticized by his old friend, then VP of marketing, who was spending more and more of his time at head office.

After a quiet period of a few weeks the first of several major shocks had hit the Dallas management team. A lengthy memo from Joan Cole contained five curt edicts:

1) Until further notice there will be no purchase orders issued from Dallas or Los Angeles. All material and supply needs will be justified to, and channeled through Baltimore. All purchasing staff in L.A. and Dallas will be terminated except for three expediters and one clerk in each location.

2) No hiring decisions (even for replacements) will be made without written approval by the CEO (Cole).

3) Production of XL73 and XZ53 (two of Thompson's best selling, but low margin, products) is to be halted pending thorough analysis of comparable products and manufacturing processes by a team of head office engineers and market specialists.

4) All employees directly and only involved in the production of XL73 and XZ53 were to be laid off, pending final product decisions.

5) All donations to local charities and causes were to be curtailed pending a policy statement for all locations.

While it is true that several new products were added at the Dallas plant, several weeks later, many of those laid off under edict item 4 were never rehired. Their expertise in XL73/XZ53 was not "adaptable to the new products."

The second major shock to the Dallas group came with the appointment of J.J. Jones, former president of the Los Angeles Chemical Corp, to the position of executive vice-president and C.O.O. Jones' new responsibilities included all production, administrative and marketing efforts. In his first week in office, Jones fired all three of the old Thompson vice-presidents. He then talked with George and asked him to accept a promotion to the position of Regional Marketing Manager. This was an entirely new position, came with a very significant raise and George would now report to the new Vice-President (Pepper) of Marketing in Baltimore who had been promoted from a sales management job within the old Franklin group. Three months later, George was required to relocate, with all of his support staff, to Baltimore. His counterpart in Los Angeles had been similarly promoted and relocated, but her support staff had quit, rather than leave the West coast.

A few months ago a major book on company policy had been distributed from Baltimore to all locations. This manual detailed all operating policies and procedures for all levels. In Dallas many people affected found the procedures quite different and hard to get used to. Some were perceived by the Texas managers to be impossible to adopt, and local suppliers and causes (including charities) were virtually cut out; a source of considerable rancor among employees with local connections.

As part of the new procedures internal audits were conducted every 3 months and though no serious disciplinary actions were taken after the first of these audits, it was clear that head office would tolerate deviances for only a brief time for adaptation. On this particular Friday George knew that his old friend in Dallas, Matt Oberlin, had just gone through an audit review. Matt was plant manager and his area of operations had been hardest hit by policy changes and lay-offs. Many of Matt's people had been around a long time. . . they found the changes very difficult to accept, and many were still hurt that some old loyal employees and friends had been laid off; many were still out of work.

As George pulled into his driveway he was not even slightly surprised when his son Ken ran out of the house to greet him - "Hi Dad! Mr. Oberlin is on the phone for you, from Dallas." "Hi, old buddy," said George, to his son, and he knew that his own discomfort would be amplified in his empathy for his friend, and that this phone call would be a miserable end to a very bad week.

***

Many topics of management could be selected for discussion and illustration of problems encountered by George and others in this case study. I have limited the selection to those which most directly can be applied to interdependence and maturity and a few of the other topics broached in this book. A Conversation about the case between Professor Barnes and Joan Pedersen (Barnes' student) now follows.

JOAN

The first thing that occurs to me as I read over this story, is that this organization seems to be excessively bureaucratic. The emphasis on written policies and edicts, the hard-nosed internal audits, the inflexibility, the centralizing efforts and the focus on efficiencies, of all sorts, Max Weber would have loved it!

BARNES

This is a good start, Joan, but we only have a vision of what is going on here through George's eyes. As you know, bureaucracy may well focus on efficiency and the other things you mentioned, but what if the problem for George and the other Thompson people is merely one of change? Change, that is from what some might consider a rather sloppy atmosphere to one in which there is desire to eliminate such sloppiness. After all, the new entity is much larger, more difficult to control.

JOAN

Certainly there is a clash of cultures here, George's discomfort is partly based on change, for sure. But there is more to it than that. George has a conviction that customer needs are paramount and that an effective organization is one which identifies customer needs and finds ways to satisfy those needs. "Open" organizations, George seems to instinctively understand, do not close out key accounts lightly, and certainly not without considering the synergy and the total client relationships. George has also been very concerned that local causes beyond the business sphere have been cut off, I mean the charities, etc. All of these things convince me that George would not be happy in the Franklin environment even if he had not experienced the "warm and fuzzy" atmosphere of Harold Thompson's operation. His attempts to communicate his convictions have failed, and his frustration in this is clearly evident, so I'm sure there is more to this than just the change.

BARNES

There are several different and powerful messages, here, each of which has something to do with maturity. First, organizations must come to realize that all business of real value is based on relationships. A relationship in which only one partner's needs are important is one which can only last so long as there is a high level of dependency by the one party. In other words, if the customer has very little choice, he will tolerate needs being only partly met by any one supplier.

This, of course, is one of the great beauties of the market. When needs are not fully being met then someone, somehow, will find a way to take advantage of the deficiency. If Franklin insists on only producing the most profitable products, not realizing that clients have a wider range of needs, then someone will (it may take a while) steal away the affected clients. The mature approach here is for Franklin to share with key clients their problems. Discuss with them the mutual need and mutually beneficial solutions. To acknowledge, openly, their mutual interdependencies.

JOAN

This might have been the way in which Franklin himself was able to get started, might it not?

BARNES

Indeed it might, but it is much more likely that it was an unconcious effort of the same sort. When you are a start-up company, or one in the earliest stages of development, there is <u>desire</u> to succeed that often overcomes a lack of understanding. If only larger firms could maintain the same level of ardent commitment to be of service! Of course, they can, but more often they become so focused on efficiency (a luxury no start-up firm can afford) that they lose sight of their intentions to provide value to clients... actually, to build relationships with clients.

JOAN

Are you saying that small firms can afford to be inefficient so long as they have high levels of commitment among employees?

BARNES

Yes, but remember that efficiency often results more from high levels of commitment than from top-down imposition of efficiency measures. Highly involved people find the best ways to accomplish virtually everything. Furthermore, they are much more likely to identify the "right" things to do. . . this we call effectiveness! I guess what I'm saying is that small firms cannot afford to <u>be</u> inefficient, they just have less reason to <u>focus</u> on it, and efficiencies occur without imposition.

The second thing to be learned from this is that maturity is not something which rests on the shoulders of only the highest ranking officials. Without trust of those whose task it is to build client relationships, trust to take care of our own interests while striving to meet client needs, there is little hope that key workers will remain enthusiastic and creative. Any ability George had, to be constantly alert to opportunities and threats in the marketplace, is being undermined completely. If he remains with Franklin, and he probably should not, it is clear that he can only do so if he becomes a "yes-man" who seeks only to be rewarded by extrinsics. He will be compliant, perhaps, but will not <u>internalize</u> the goals and methods of the firm.

JOAN

As you were speaking of these things, it occurred to me that Franklin in its early days, Thompson in recent years and Franklin now, are examples of the various phases of growth and organizational crisis as depicted by Larry Greiner. Either Franklin, in its early days, experienced growth "through creativity," (Greiner's Phase 1) or by buying already existing firms it bypassed that phase. Certainly Thompson's company, a textbook "power culture" had been in some early stage of development and had not reached the crisis of Leadership, the second phase in Greiner's model. By contrast, Franklin did experience the crisis of Leadership and hired "the much-needed professional manager." Now, they are experiencing the crisis of red tape after going through Greiner's growth phase four. Do you think all organizations necessarily go through all the Greiner Phases?

BARNES

Probably not, or if they do, there are different levels of crisis manifestation. In the Franklin case, to illustrate, the delegation phase (No.3) has been by-passed as their organization grew through acquisition, as you noted. Remember, this is an invented case study to stimulate your attempts to apply these theories. Certainly you are correct in your analysis. Franklin can emerge from their current crisis, as Greiner suggests, by emphasizing coordination which, by the way is nothing but an acknowledgement of the interdependencies inherent in my notion of maturity. Just how long it takes for this to happen depends on many variables. Franklin will not emerge from this crisis, certainly, unless they realize that it is indeed a crisis. If their methods "work," that is if they continue to operate profitably, continue to grow, continue to be described by industry analysts as "efficient," they may never mature. High levels of turnover and other affective failures will never be strong stimulus for change.

JOAN

It would take marketplace pressures, wouldn't it? But can a firm remain moderately successful for significant periods of time before the marketplace itself matures and brings about the necessary pressure for change?

BARNES

Indeed! In fact whole industries can be so recalcitrant. If all actors within an olygopolistic industry (like the American Automobile industry, for example) remain intransigent and moderately interested in customer satisfaction, then all can go on in that manner for a very long time indeed.

Of course a monopoly is also a condition which, as I said earlier, "permits" the sole or very strong major player, to remain essentially in a crisis without realizing it (IBM?). It takes a major external threat to make the crisis apparent. The currently fluctuating economic conditions are mediating variables, of course, as are social changes of all sorts, and technological sub-

stitutions. The auto industry fell asleep and
remained that way partly because no substitute emerged and the competitive threat was
relatively late on the scene.

JOAN

You said there were other things to be
learned from my comments about bureauc-
racies and cultures.

BARNES

Yes, well one other thing which occurs to
me is that communications with people on
every level inside the old Thompson
Company (by Franklin before the merger)
would have been very wise. I do mean
communications! Two-way, open discussions designed to provide several things.
First of all, vital information gained about
Thompson's employees themselves. It is
absolutely immature to assume that a sales
manager in one culture (that is one who is
effective in one culture) is automatically a
potential sales manager in another. No
sane manager would hire an employee, on
virtually any level, without meeting that
person and attempting to understand
something of their strengths. Yet this is
exactly what Franklin did, they hired a
whole lot of people they had never met!

It is also abundantly clear that Franklin has
no idea what kind of culture exists within

its own organization. This, in itself, is a form of immaturity. How can a meaningful mission be developed without a keen appreciation of the strengths we have? And the weaknesses!

Franklin assumed, then delivered on the basis of that assumption, that new people "hired" in the acquisition would simply fit or be dumped.

The other important information gained from interviewing key employees before the merger is that having to do with relationships with customers and suppliers.

Another thing to be observed about change is that successful change, of individuals or collectives, is that it takes time. There are several change "models" in the academic literature, they all have many common elements, the most important being the creation of open communications.

JOAN

Can I go back again to the possibility you admitted that George might simply be immature himself, that his supposition is right: he had merely been (with Thompson) under that paternal protection of the "old man." If this is true, and he was really quite dependent, he may not have matured sufficiently to tolerate high pressure to perform on a more independent basis.

BARNES

Well, let's look at the evidence. . .
George certainly has shown signs of frustration. He regresses, emotionally, living in a past time, longing for a return to the comforts of his prior setting. These are certainly signs of immaturity, but two very important counterpoints. First, in the old Thompson operation new product development was based on "colaborative efforts among insiders, suppliers and customers." This is the epitome of mature interdependence. Second, maturity is not a state which anyone reaches then remains mature under all circumstances. Anyone can regress under pressure. The point is that George is not being mentored at this critical juncture. He has been promoted, relocated and confronted with a cultural frontier all at the same time. He has also had his personal ties severed and now, more than ever, he needs a strong mentor; someone he can trust completely and in whom he can find trust. Instead, all he gets is admonishment and edict!

JOAN

You mentioned communications problems and specifically the need to communicate prior to the merger. It seems to me that the written notices (post-merger) from Cole are also problematic. Is it because authority is being removed from George, and others, or is it the impersonal nature of the communication that is most galling?

BARNES

It is the combination of these two and something else. Written memo's are a terrible way to communicate with anyone for whom you have respect, especially when the information comes as a surprise. Cole and George are in the same location, same building, probably... there is just no excuse for this lapse. All recipients of these memo's (if they have to exist at all, which is questionable) should have been given opportunity to provide input and influence to the decision process behind the edicts. Why have managers on the payroll if the key people, on their own, know everything and can make all decisions for others to enact?

The impersonality is an exacerbating variable, but George, and any other manager who feels competent, is bound to resent exclusion from the process. This might be especially true since George had definitely been included in the Thompson company.

JOAN

Surely George's "other" roles in life are under some kind of pressure here too? He must be feeling some discomfort on the personal level.

BARNES

Undoubtedly! Information in the case suggests that George's wife has adapted well to the change, and so have the children. But this may be part of the problem. If George's family adapts well, and he does not, this becomes a considerable irritant to George. Often the reverse pattern is experienced when employees are relocated. The challenge of multiple roles of employees, the realization that people have lives outside the organization are manifestations of acknowledged interdependencies by organizational leaders. Striving for the highest levels of bureaucratic efficiency and control without respect for personal difficulties being experienced is a sure sign of an immature organization.

Regarding the foregoing discussion: I acknowledge that meeting with employees of a merger target, before a merger, presents some real challenges of impropriety. In some cases such meetings may not be possible. However, there is no reason to delay communications of the sort implied here more than one day after the merger is accomplished. It should be priority #1! In any event, the message here is an important one, whenever "hiring" anyone, through merger or more traditional means, it is imperative that the hiring process includes a full disclosure about the workplace, its mission, culture, goals and policies. To do less is equivalent to not expecting full disclosure from a job applicant, something no mature manager would tolerate.

EPILOGUE

Readers, by now, must know that I see the full development of the human resource as the key to organizational success. Further, you know that behaviors recommended throughout this manual I see as the fundamental keys to Management Maturity. This, in turn, leads to the creation of an environment which serves to provide stimuli and rewards (for the behaviors recommended), for active mentoring on all levels, and in which people not only feel excited to be involved, but also in which risk-taking is celebrated - errors/mistakes seen by leaders as positive signs that the organization itself is mature.

Johnson and Johnson, one of America's "best-run" companies is an organization which has progressed toward this state and James Burke, former CEO says of this mature environment that it is, at once, a place where people feel "free" to make mistakes, but, because they do, and because of the "climate" engendered, very few mistakes are actually made.

To reach the level indicated in the Johnson and Johnson story takes much time, great patience and the strict adherence to the general tenets of the guidelines contained in this book - BUT AT ALL LEVELS, NO EXCEPTIONS!

But there is another requirement, one not spelled out previously in the foregoing pages. It relates, directly to Mentoring, but it goes substantially further. I refer to the active coaching of people who show promise and interest in their own career paths and options.

Many organizations are relatively good at asking young managers a question which goes something like this: "Mary (or John, or?), what kinds of things would you like to be doing next (or in five years, or. . .)?" The context for this line of questioning is, often, the final phases of the "annual performance review." It has a nice paternal ring to it, it seems an appropriate way to motivate someone who is progressing well and it gives "the boss" a good opportunity to inject the subtle reminder that he/she is the one who will influence further career moves (a power reminder).

A far better approach to the development of high-potential people would be for "the boss" to take the time and trouble to draw several road-maps for the protege. These maps should be relatively concrete (that is based on reality rather than fantasy) and should be based on the strengths of the candidate and the real needs for the positions included in the next two or three steps of the identified pathways.

As part of this diagraming of possibilities, obviously, "the boss" should have discussed the various steps in the pathways identified with his/her own boss and several other managers - to ensure a full understanding of what it would take for someone to succeed in each of the several positions involved.

This, then, for each person judged to be promotable the organization should provide several alternative plans. Remember, a plan is a series of decisions made "in advance." Like all plans, there are contingencies. One of your (boss) responsibilities is to describe, fairly and frankly, the kinds of developmental changes the protege would need to make (growth goals) in order to be given the opportunity and in order to have a chance of succeeding in the realized path.

An organization in which people are striving hard to be the best they can be in their current assignment and also have several relatively clear and specific next steps to prepare for, is one with maximized human potentials. I can assure readers that such an organization - but one which follows through with the plans most of the time - is one which will invent its own quality. That is quality products, quality processes, quality relationships with customers, suppliers and all "stakeholders." Such an organization is one any one of us would find exciting and one that will find ways to compete successfully in its markets. Such a result is possible in any organization, but the first step, always must be in developing widespread MANAGEMENT MATURITY through acknowledgement of interdependencies.

In a last-ditch effort to persuade readers, and to increase the credibility of my ideas and this manual I will close with two direct quotations from other "experts."

In a recent issue of the Academy of Management Review, 17, 3, 1992, author Aktouf - one of many academics who feel, as I do, that the various forms of "interdependence" contain the keys to organizational futures with maximized potentials, says:

There is a clear need to abandon management based on authority, on an order imposed by the organization, on the successive waves of scientism that have invaded the field (e.g., Taylorism, behavioral sciences, decision making, management information systems, office systems and robotics). The solution is to open the way for managerial practices that will permit development of the employee's desire to belong and to use his or her intelligence to serve the firm.

Such practices will never be conceived unless radical questions are asked about what, until now, has apparently been the major stumbling block; the conception (and treatment) of the worker as an instrument of production, as some sort of "needs-driven" mechanism, as a rational and avid maximizer of profits, as a resource to be exploited and monitored and as a cost to be controlled and minimized.

. . . Hence, it now seems imperative to [sic] find a transition from a form of management in which the employee is seen as a passive cog, to one in which he or she becomes an active and willing accomplice. This almost complete reversal of roles might lead to the heights of liberation or to the pit of alienation and exploitation. But recognition of the need to promote the worker (forcibly implying more respect for his or her interest and autonomy), even if from a strictly managerial and economic perspective is, I believe,

already a big step forward. The worker's increased autonomy is inconceivable without some sharing of power, of
management decision-making rights, and of rights over
means, profits and so forth.

And from Stephen R. Covey (Author of The Seven Habits of
Highly Effective People) comes the following:

Interdependence is the ability to not only see the larger
picture, but to successfully negotiate within it, cope with it
and optimize. Very few people are trained in interdependency. Most of us are heavily trained and scripted in independency. The problem is that we are acting independently
in an interdependent reality. It's like playing tennis with a
golf club. But you know it's so easy to talk of interdependency and very difficult to live it in a sustained way.
It requires an abundance mentality and a real inner security.

I agree with Professor Aktouf, though I am not naive about the
important potentials for organizations to become more effective
through careful adaptation of new technologies. This is, indeed, the
age of information; but the human component will always be the
essential key.

I find Dr. Covey's statement especially apt and am convinced
that the needed cultural change within organizations, the "inner security" Covey prescribes, calls for a total commitment to the concepts
and the practices I call MANAGEMENT MATURITY.   Try it,
you'll like the results!

Index

166 *Index*

ABOUT THE AUTHOR

Dr. A. Keith Barnes is a relatively unusual academic - he has "been there" in the areas in which he teaches and about which this book is written. His career in business spanned twenty-five years, during which there was not one major functional area to which he was not exposed. Beginning as an engineer in mining and minerals extraction he moved through sales and marketing, manufacturing and distribution to policy-level management in domestic and international environments. After considerable experience at the senior ranks (Regional General Manager) with Tenneco's J.I. Case Company, he decided to become an academic. He holds MBA and doctoral degrees in management from Pepperdine University and has served on two corporate boards of directors. He teaches Management and Policy at the University of Redlands (a selective private institution in California) where he has held for several years the prestigious S.V. Hunsaker Endowed Chair in Management. In 1989 he was chosen "Professor of the Year" at Redlands.

Barnes served as Management Editor of the Journal of Applied Business Research from 1988 to 1992. He is now on the Editorial Board for that journal and for the Journal of Management Systems. He has published nationally and internationally in academic journals on mentoring, management, policy and related topics. Management Maturity: Prerequisite to Total Quality is Barnes' first book.